Echoes of
Past Lives:
True Hauntings
of the South

May all your ghosts be friendly!

Ronn L Nyfa

Echoes of Past Lives: True Hauntings of the South

by
Ronnie L. Nixon
Shaun P. Nichols
Philip B. Brownell

Printed in Victoria, Canada

National Library of Canada Cataloguing in Publication

Nixon, Ronnie L., 1948-
 Echoes of past lives : true hauntings of the South /
Ronnie L. Nixon, Shaun P. Nichols, Philip B. Brownell.
ISBN 1-55395-113-1
 I. Nichols, Shaun P. II. Brownell, Philip B.
III. Title.
BF1472.U6N59 2002   133.1'0975   C2002-904417-0

TRAFFORD

This book was published *on-demand* in cooperation with Trafford Publishing.
On-demand publishing is a unique process and service of making a book available for retail sale to the public taking advantage of on-demand manufacturing and Internet marketing.
On-demand publishing includes promotions, retail sales, manufacturing, order fulfilment, accounting and collecting royalties on behalf of the author.

2404 Government St., Victoria, B.C. V8T 4L7, CANADA
Phone   250-383-6864   Toll-free   1-888-232-4444 (Canada & US)
Fax   250-383-6804   E-mail   sales@trafford.com
Web site   www.trafford.com   TRAFFORD PUBLISHING IS A DIVISION OF TRAFFORD HOLDINGS LTD.
Trafford Catalogue #02-0827   www.trafford.com/robots/02-0827.html

10   9   8   7   6   5   4   3   2   1

<u>Dedication</u>

To Vickie, Gavin, Lee, and Trever who are the source of my inspiration
                                    Ronnie L. Nixon

To Shannon, Noah, and my family who supported my passion for paranormal research
                                    Philip B. Brownell

To my wife Stephanie and my family who have stood behind me and encouraged me throughout my paranormal investigations
                                    Shaun P. Nichols

Table of Contents

Preface

Recently a local radio station was doing its morning trivia question. "A poll was conducted that revealed a full 70% of those questioned had a common experience. What was it?" After about thirty minutes of guesses ranging from "having prayers answered" to "being rudely treated at the grocery store checkout counter," the answer was: "70% of those questioned admitted to seeing a ghost or had a paranormal experience on one or more occasions." This came as a complete surprise. Is the number really that high? But when one thinks about it, why would it not be. If ghosts truly are spirits of the dead caught between the "world of the living" and the "other side," there certainly have been an abundance of opportunities throughout history.

The Alabama Foundation for Paranormal Research (AFFPR) is one of several like groups around the country dedicated to investigating sites known to have demonstrated "ghostly" paranormal activity. This activity may take forms such as ghost lights, apparitions, sounds, smells, or radical temperature changes that all appear to emanate from no apparent source. Although there has been and continues to be serious scientific inquiry into these various phenomena, the quest to capture a photograph or videotape of an apparition or a voice on tape is one of the fastest growing hobbies in the United States. Consequently there has been a proliferation of internet web sites and publications showing off the results of the investigations.

In fiction ghosts are almost always full-body apparitions that appear and disappear seemingly at will to the unsuspecting living. Ghosts do manifest themselves in this way. However, there are other manifestations that are much more frequent in occurrence. Orbs or glowing balls of light that are mostly transparent, vortexes or columns of light that swirl, and ectoplasm or misty apparitions are the others. All of the possibilities are seen by photographic means when they can't be seen by the naked eye.

In addition to visible evidence the presence of ghosts can be detected by the sounds they make, the smells they leave, or by feel. The various experiences related in this work will contain examples of all of these.

In this book we have honestly conveyed all that we have seen and have experienced on our investigations that cannot be explained as ordinary at the different locations. We have diligently reviewed and re-reviewed all our information, and whenever there was any doubt in our minds that the phenomena could be explained as normal, it was eliminated. There are many who simply dismiss all of these phenomena as explainable in one way or another. For example EVPs (electronic voice phenomena) are said to actually be bleed in from radio transmissions into the recorder. We certainly would not pretend to believe that this could not or would not happen. However, it is hard to believe that a paranormal investigator standing alone in an open field where a battle with great loss of life was fought nearly a century and a half ago, capturing a voice that clearly relates to a military maneuver is experiencing radio bleed in. It's too simple an explanation for the hundreds of EVPs have been captured in like manner. This explanation would only hold if the majority of the voices are unrelated to the scene at hand.

We consider our ghost hunts to be serious undertakings, and we adhere strictly to the *Standards and Protocols* of the International Ghost Hunters Society that were written to provide a guideline to ensure hunts are done with proper respect and with a high degree of honesty and integrity. The Standards and Protocols are:

1. Ask the spirits of the dead for permission to take their pictures

2. No smoking tobacco products during an investigation
3. No alcohol before, during or after an investigation if remaining on site
4. No Ouija boards or séances during or after an investigation if on site
5. Always conduct your investigations in a professional manner
6. Respect posted property, ask permission and do not trespass
7. Do not take photographs during adverse weather conditions
8. Adverse weather conditions are rain, mist, fog, snow, windy/dusty conditions
9. Do not take photos from moving vehicles on dusty roads
10. Do not take photos while walking on dusty roads
11. Remove all dust, spots, fingerprints from camera lens
12. Remove or wear the camera strap so it does not hang loose
13. Avoid shooting into the sun for resulting lens flare
14. Avoid shooting with flash at reflective or shiny surfaces
15. Keep fingers away from the lens of the camera
16. Keep long hair away from the lens of the camera
17. Avoid shooting when foreign objects are floating near camera

18. No running or horse play in cemeteries or historical sites
19. Show reverence and respect in cemeteries, battlefields, etc.
20. Always use fresh audio tapes for EVP recordings
21. Compare anomalous prints with negatives for confirmation
22. Flash is only good for 9-12 feet from camera so focus on that range
23. Positive mental attitude is very important for all investigations
24. Skeptical minds will generate negative energy during an investigation
25. Follow the IGHS cycles for conducting investigations for best results

So, now let's go on a journey with the ghost hunters of the AFFPR. It has been a fun ride for us, and we truly hope it will be for you.

Ronnie, Phillip, and Shaun

<u>Acknowledgements</u>

We wish to thank and respectfully acknowledge all the members of the AFFPR both past and present for their contributions to our investigations. Jamie Cutler, Chris Vickers, Courtney McGraw, Wayne McGraw, Becky Kimbrell, Adam Kimbrell, Jason Hastings, and Matt Hudson have all been invaluable to this work.

In addition the following people were instrumental in facilitating this publication because they were so kind as to open their doors to us and to provide background information on the various sites: Chris & Tracy Maze, Denise Resler and the Board of Directors of the Whole Backstage Theater, The Staff of Russell Cave, Patti and Darwin Palmer, and Rhonda and Tommy Mills.

14

HAUNTED CHURCHES

Worship for the Weary

Nestled in a shallow valley about one hundred yards off the side of a long, dark, country road in middle Tennessee is an old abandoned gothic-style church.[1]   Just by driving by and seeing this building, there is no way to tell that it is actually a former place of worship.   Churches have crosses atop their steeples. This church has an object that looks like a hand of some sort holding a crystal ball. The windows are painted blood red. The only way to enter is in the front of the building. At the top of the building is a bell tower, but there are no stairs or any other obvious means of gaining access. The church pews that occupy the building are at least twelve feet long and weigh by best estimate at least three hundred pounds.

This church is believed to have been a secret lodge at one time, and there are local rumors that several illicit hangings were conducted in the trees that surround the building.   Perhaps the strangest of these hangings took place in the bell tower of all places. Other rumors have it that perversions

---

[1] Since this church is privately owned and has been the subject of previous vandalism, we have decided not to reveal the name of the church or its location. We do this out of respect for those who allow us to do our investigations.

also took place upstairs where it is said that many young women were abused in various ways at the hands of the men.

Many people have experienced the paranormal here, and some have had multiple experiences. Probably one of the oddest sightings that has been reported is an apparition of a woman pushing a baby carriage around in the front yard of the church. Also, it has been reported that at times one can see an apparition of the person that was hung in the bell tower. Others have become nauseated either just before stepping foot on the property or once actually in the church. Another common sight that people have witnessed is a cobweb-like figure of a man hunched over in one of the corners inside the sanctuary. Some of the locals have said that they have seen a black figure in the window while they were driving by. They would stop their vehicle, go up to the church, and no one would be inside. Stories like these drive people to these places, and many times they find out what they would really prefer not knowing.

We have had the honor of investigating this place on two separate occasions. The first was in September of 2001. A group of six of us had heard legends and rumors about this haunted church. In fact some of the rumors were almost too good to be true for a group of ghost hunters. So in order to find out for ourselves, we made the trip. We parked about

150 yards from the building and walked. Because waist-high grass surrounded the place, parking near the church was not an option. We proceeded to the church, and noted that the exterior certainly looked like it belonged in England. The structure and appearance were one of a very old Gothic setting. Anyone driving this road would have known this was an odd location for such a structure. As we had heard before the windows were painted blood red, and it is difficult to see inside just by driving by or even by standing in front of the windows.

Anxious now that we had finally made it, armed with the legends and rumors surrounding this building, and with our equipment, we made our way inside. One could easily tell that this place had not been in use for a very long time. Dust covered the pews and the floor. After about 30 minutes into our visit, we started noting some activity. We first picked up a few orbs. Most of these were at the wall near the entrance. From other paranormal field reports this is where a cobwebbed figure had been seen. As time passed we continued to capture more activity.

The strangest thing (and one that we will never forget) about that hunt was that as we were nearing the end of our investigation one of the guys who had tagged along for the hunt stood staring out the window and would not respond to anyone. We were taking pictures and getting readings from our other equipment when we noticed that someone was standing at the back window. At first glance it looked like an apparition, but it stood there too long. So we started a roll call for each person to respond to verify that they were here. When we got to the last person, we called out their name, and there was no response. So not believing that he didn't answer, we called it again. Again there was no response. Finally after a few minutes that person walked away from the window and started speaking to us as if nothing had happened. We asked him what he was doing just standing there gazing out the window into space. He said he was at ease when he was there, and he didn't really notice that his behavior was particularly odd. As it turns out that was the same location in the church where the figure was seen and where we got most of our paranormal activity. We didn't go into the bell tower on that night because no matter how hard we searched there was just no access available. Others say there is a hidden entrance, but we were not able to locate it.

Our second trip to the church was in mid-October of 2001. At that time there were ten of us that went along for the investigation.

Gigantic orb photographed inside the gothic church.

The word had gotten out that this was the place to be for a ghost hunter. We parked in the same general location as we did for the first hunt. As we approached the church one of our friends who had come along became very nauseated. This turned out to be a common occurrence during that visit. In fact some were so sick that they never left the car. Luckily, however, one, although nauseated, was able to continue on the hunt with us. The grass around the church seemed to have grown to the point that it now was a couple of inches above our waist. As we neared the church, we started taking pictures from the outside. This night the paranormal activity heated up quickly. In our first few pictures we picked up considerable orb activity around the bell tower where we had not spent much time during the previous trip.

We made our way inside and right away the feeling that someone was watching came over most of us. The person who had been feeling nauseous was now feeling worse. We had our digital cameras, still cameras, thermal meters, night vision scopes, infrared detectors and sound recorders all going simultaneously it seemed. In most cases of paranormal activity of the type typical of this church it is very rare to see orbs, mist, ectoplasm, or apparitions with the naked eye. On this occasion it was no different. The night vision scope was required. One could gaze through the scope and see the orbs dancing against the back wall. To verify what we were seeing we would take pictures of the location, and sure enough, the orbs could be seen by both instruments as verification of their existence (instead of dust motes which are often mistaken for orbs). Shortly another member of the group became extremely nauseated. Someone was coughing outside, and a couple of people went out to check on him. When they got there, he was standing on the front steps with a washed-out look. He was asked if he was ok and he stated that he didn't really know what had happened. One moment he was looking through the night vision scope and the next moment he was very weak and sick. Now there were two out of the ten who were experiencing nausea. This feeling was also described as one of total energy loss. One can barely walk and can only communicate with difficulty.

As the night progressed things began to get even stranger. We were all in the middle aisle of the church with pews on both sides. They were aligned in rows of about ten pews that are nearly ten foot long and probably about 300 pounds. While we were standing there relating other legends that we had heard about the church, we decided to try to communicate with the spirits that were in this place. We asked some general questions to see if we could elicit a response. When we said "If you are in here, please show yourself," one of the heavy pews moved up. The first thought was that someone in our group had moved it, but everyone was in the center aisle with no opportunity to have done it without being noticed. To the person everyone confirmed that they had not been the one to have moved the pew. Actually there was no way to move it even if we really wanted to do so considering the weight. It was simply too heavy for the average person to attempt to move alone. Our sound recorders had been on at the time, and we captured the sound of the pew scraping against the floor as it moved.

Again as during the last hunt the orbs were visible in our night vision scope, and we captured them on camera to verify what we were seeing. One of the oddest things that showed up in the photographs was a cross in one of the windows. One in our group had taken a snapshot of the window just to the right of the choir seats, and in one of the window frames a cross appeared. When they took another picture of the same window, the cross was gone. Another thing conspicuous in most of our photographs was the presence of black and white hues. This has been interpreted by some to be a battle of good and evil.

On this trip we made another effort to find the hidden entrance to the bell tower but were still not able to do so. We did find what appeared to be a pull down ladder, but it was in the ceiling and was not reachable.

As we took a walk around the outside of the building to determine the level of paranormal activity present there, the last person in the line kept saying they had a feeling that someone was behind them. This is a very common feeling that many have reported experiencing here. We went to the right side of the church and noticed bars at the foundation level. A couple of us got on hands and knees and shined our lights underneath to see if we could see anything unusual there. It was pitch black. No matter how you shined your light there you could see absolutely nothing. It was like a bottomless pit that was occupied by complete darkness. We found this fact interesting but didn't place much value on it considering the fact that that kind of phenomenon can be easily explained by light-absorbing materials of construction.

So deciding that there was nothing below, we went back inside for another go at it. As we were nearing the end of the night's investigation, we had noticed someone again standing and staring out the back window as if in a trance. Although we called his name at least three times, he did not respond, and it took several minutes before he would turn around to acknowledge us. We asked him what he was doing, and he said he felt at ease gazing out the window. Déjà vu. This was exactly what had happened on our first visit but to a different person who had not been on that trip and who knew nothing of the occurrence. Some paranormal researchers interpret this as being at the threshold of a portal into another dimension where one's energy drains rapidly, and it becomes very difficult to emerge. This type of occurrence is strong evidence for not performing paranormal investigations alone but always in pairs. If one becomes entranced, the other can be there to help them emerge. Other visual evidence during our investigation proved that corner of the church to be the most active location.

Spirits or ghosts have a way of trying to warn people. That night two in our group became very sick. The first person to become sick was the only African-American that was there. We believe that he may very well have become so sick because of the lynchings that had taken place there so many years before. Maybe the spirits of those who were unjustly treated at the hands of those who were so bigoted and cruel were warning him away from the place of the ultimate cruelty. This was obviously a place of great pain and suffering, and to us it was a place of great sadness. The pain experienced there had a profound effect on all of us. The second person to get sick was experiencing this pain in empathy with those who so many years before first experienced it.

Ectoplasm just above one of the investigators

On our two trips to the church we did not experience all that was rumored to occur there at different times. However, with the photographs, sound recordings, feelings, and the various experiences we had, everyone that participated in the investigations left believing that something paranormal was definitely going on in this one-time place of worship.

While many people have had numerous unsuccessful trips to this church in terms of witnessing firsthand the level of paranormal activity, the only two times we visited the place we were not disappointed. Maybe it was the respect that we showed the place, or maybe it was the methods we used during our investigations. Regardless of the reason we walked away from the church as believers in a many of the legends, and we are eager to return to this place of Gothic horror.

07/10/2002

The Congregation Still Gathers

The very first adventure during which we encountered a haunted church was on a small and winding road in the middle of nowhere in southern Tennessee. The outward appearance is that of an abandoned, white clapboard church with a graveyard across the road from it once used as a place of worship by many of the families in this small unincorporated community.[2] Records indicate that it was probably the second Methodist church to be started in the area. The records also indicate that the graveyard was established in 1815. Based on that information and local lore we determined that the church was probably established only a few years before that, and it was once a regular meeting place for families and friends in this small and quiet community.

Legend has it that one Sunday night in the early 1800's while a service was going on out of nowhere a hirsute beast entered the church. No one had ever seen this creature, man, or whatever it was around the community before. Without saying a word the creature went back outside, nailed the single entrance door shut, and burned the building to the ground killing what was estimated to be at least forty people. The bodies were buried across the street in a cemetery that took its name from the church. There are many graves there marked only with stones having no inscriptions that may be evidence of such an event.

Thinking that the evil spirit or creature had finished his unholy business on a holy people, the community decided to rebuild the church in the same location within only a few years. Time passed and everything seemed

---

[2] In an attempt to preserve the church and to keep away unwanted visitors we have decided not to reveal the name or location of this church.

normal until a few years later when another devastating event occurred. On April 29, 1909 a tornado struck on a day that appeared to one of the nicest days of the spring and demolished the church. A few of the church members who lived nearby were killed when the tornado struck their houses, and they were buried in the cemetery across the road from the church.

This time only a year or so passed by before the community would try it once again. They rebuilt the church and tried to take a different approach to try to avert any other disasters from befalling this house of God. The devout members of the church decided to bless and place a bible inside to ward off any evil that might come their way. There was only one small problem that they were facing. Everyone in the area was aware of the two incidents that had devastated the church and of the many lives that were lost and decided not to attend services there. The church was jinxed. Of course no church can survive without the tithes and offerings from the people, so services were forced to discontinue. To this very day, the white church with the Bible, an old artesian well, and a graveyard still occupy the same location. So do the spirits of many of the poor souls who met their demise there.

It is a mystery why some ghosts or spirits only reveal themselves to certain people. Many believe that it is a gift to be able to see apparitions, and others believe that apparitions are mere illusions. Probably most of the time the spirits or ghosts are trying to convey a message to the person or maybe a message through them for someone else.

When we first laid eyes on this church, we thought that the local legends that we had heard were merely myths. There are no lights anywhere around and only one house within a couple of miles. At first glance it would appear that services still take place in the building except there is no indication outside of what denomination it is or when services are held. However, we later found that it is only used on special occasions. There haven't been any field investigations reported by any other paranormal groups, so all we had to go on were tales from the locals who had heard about this place. On our first few trips there we didn't have much luck in detecting significant paranormal activity in either the cemetery or in the church. We did happen to catch some orbs on film though, and this is what brought us back for further investigation.

On our fourth trip we began discovering many other things out of the ordinary besides orbs. In front of the church is an artesian well. Artesian wells flow constantly due to underground air pressure placed on the natural water reservoir there. This particular well had somehow earned the name "cold waters of hell," and it didn't take us long to figure out why. No one really knew how far underground the water was that was coming to the surface here, but they knew it was coming from underground. However, the water that was flowing out of the pipe was by far some of the coldest natural water we had ever touched. While we were walking toward the sidewalk leading to the church, we noticed that the water changed its speed of flow. So we walked backwards a couple of steps, and the flow returned to normal again. We experimented with the same pattern of walking towards the sidewalk and taking a couple steps back, and we got the same result each time. We walked over to the water and started speaking to it. Here we were actually talking to water, but something was definitely out of the ordinary so our actions were out of the ordinary also. We would ask questions at the well to see if we could get a response by a change in the flow rate. We said the words "We know you can stop the water, we want to see the water stop." No sooner had those words been said the water flow dropped to zero as if a spigot had been turned off. It stopped for about 2 seconds, and then returned to normal where it stayed for the rest of the evening.

We made our way to the front of the church and peeked inside the windows. The inside looked to be in good condition except for the dust that covered the pews and floors. We went to the side of the building where we heard a very strange noise. It sounded like a rattle.

Listening closer, we heard the sound of a chain dragging. It was like a drag across the leaves. We stood there in silence hoping we would hear it again, but after about ten minutes we decided to move on. We made our way around the church and noticed some glowing objects in the trees. They were green in color and were stationary. They would fade in and out, so we were able to take a couple of photographs. After about five minutes of observing them they faded out.

Eager to see what we could find at the cemetery across the street, we went to the entrance gate. As we got to the gate we heard a high-pitched scream. It sounded like a woman in trouble. Since we didn't hear it again, we passed it off as probably a bobcat which is an animal that is prevalent in this area of the South. We viewed the cemetery from the knee-high brick wall. After about five minutes we encountered one of the most incredible phenomena. We were staring into the cemetery, and no more than ten feet in front of us there appeared a cloaked figure. It appeared to be over six and a half feet tall and had a black, shadowy cloak. We could not distinguish any facial features. It appeared and said "LEAVE." Those of us who had seen it took its advice. We joined the rest of the group, and decided that we had better end the investigation for that evening. We do not know who the figure was or why it appeared. Probably it was trying to warn us or to tell us something. Whatever the case may be its' point was very clear that there had been enough investigating for that night.

On our way home something else very strange happened. The smell of gasoline became very strong inside the car. We thought that maybe the car was leaking, but we noticed the smell was coming from our hands. As we checked it more, it was coming only from the hands that we had used to touch the water from the well. The smell of gasoline only remained for a minute or so and then faded away. We later found out that this water is normal water that is used for drinking by many people in the community who regularly stop by to fill their containers.

The artesian well

36

A week or so passed before we assembled another group to go back to the church. Many were anxious to see the cloaked figure. So the first place we went this time was the brick wall of the cemetery. We stood there in hopes that this apparition would make another appearance, but it didn't happen. Accepting the fact that it wasn't going to appear for us at that time, we went over to the artesian well. We took a different approach to study the flow of the water. A couple from the group went to the front door while others stayed out by the well. We did a series of knocks on the door and watched for what would happen. After knocking a few times, the water came nearly to a complete stop and stayed this way for a couple of minutes before returning to regular speed.

While tapping on the door we discovered that we had been getting a response other than from the water. As soon as we would knock on the door we would get a reply with a tap on the window. It wasn't a strong tap. It was one that sounded much like someone that had long fingernails was making a light tap on the window with them. After notifying the rest of the group, we went over to the window and shined our lights inside, but no one was there. As a matter of fact is was impossible for anyone to have gotten into the building. One door was padlocked, and the others were nailed shut. The tapping continued throughout the time that we were there and would follow us as we moved from place to place and window to window around the church. We discussed the last investigation when we heard the sound of the chain rattling so we listened carefully as we made our way to that side of the church. We said, "This is where we heard it last time" to try to get a response but did not hear it this time. However, there was a window directly to our backs, and we began to hear the tapping there. We turned around, took a peek inside the window, and saw a glowing ball dancing on the floor. Initially we thought it was a reflection of something from the equipment we were carrying, but we had no light source that night. With digital cameras we were able to capture it as it moved back and forth across the floor. It appeared to be similar to the ones we had seen in the trees, and just like those this one blinked out after only a few minutes.

At the back of the church we used the night vision scopes. This was the darkest location so we figured we would have better results. Eager to find something, we turned the corner of the church and sure enough something caught our eye in the cemetery across the road. It appeared to be one of the brick columns there. As we looked closer though, we noticed that it was moving back and forth. We focused on the other column next to it, and what we were seeing was a couple of feet taller than the column itself. The cloaked figure had made a return, but this time it appeared that it was guarding something. That something was the entrance to the cemetery. We have often wondered why we have only spotted him on the cemetery side of the wall and not on the church side.

On our way back home from the church we reviewed some of the tapes that we had made, and we found something astonishing. Although we did not hear a chain rattle that night when we were at the side of the church, something sounding like a rattle can be definitely heard on the videotape. One important thing that we have learned from our investigations is that just because you actually do not hear or see anything while on location does not mean you haven't captured something with the recording equipment.

On subsequent visits we have had a number of different phenomena to occur. It seems that the more we return the more active the site becomes. We have now become so familiar with the church and its surroundings that we now know where and what to look for, but this place never ceases to amaze us in what it has to offer. On our next investigation we heard a very loud scream. It sounded like a wild animal. However, as we kept listening it grew much louder until it seemed that screams were coming from all around us. They lasted for a total of about 2 minutes, and everyone in the group heard them clearly. The recorders were on so we were hopeful that we recorded them.   Immediately after the screaming stopped, we reviewed our tapes. Amazingly we didn't record any screams.   What we had recorded was the sound of a woman's voice saying, "HELP ME."   We played it over many times to make sure we were hearing what we thought.   Sure enough the whole group confirmed it.

Later we went to the wall of the cemetery and climbed over.   About five feet into the cemetery, the temperature dropped nearly fifteen degrees, but it only seemed to do so in one area of the graveyard. We walked to spots where we felt warmer and then walked back to the spot where we were experiencing the cold, and sure enough, it wasn't our imagination.   It is believed that cold spots indicate that a spirit or ghost is present. Although you may not be able to see them, temperature changes are one way to tell that they are with you.

Our investigation that night proved to be very successful. We captured very large orbs on film inside the graveyard, church, and on the road, but our friend, the black cloaked figure, did not make a return visit.

Keeping an open mind and being willing to accept your findings is a key to paranormal investigations.   In the paranormal there are many ways that the spirits and ghosts manifest themselves and communicate with us. More often than not it may take several trips for confirmation of paranormal activity at a given location. Our experiences here covered the range of changes in the flow of water, tapping at the windows and doors, a woman's voice, and the appearance of the cloaked apparition. What was the woman was trying to tell us? Why does the cloaked figure still roam the cemetery? One thing is certain: even though the services have discontinued here, the congregation still gathers.

HAUNTED CAVES

The entrance to Russell Cave showing the upper level to
the right and the stream passage to the left

Looking out of the cave entrance

The Natives of Russell Cave

Russell Cave near Bridgeport in the northeastern corner of Alabama was excavated by a team of archeologists and anthropologists sponsored by the Smithsonian Institution and the National Geographic Society in the mid-1950's. It was rediscovered by the Chattanooga Chapter of the Tennessee Archeological Society in 1953 after almost 500 years of being lost preceded by more than eight thousand years of prehistoric usage. Two locations in the upper level of the cave yielded a large number of tools, weapons, and animal bones as well as three complete and three partial human skeletons that resulted from occupancy by prehistoric hunters and gatherers. The Park Rangers tell us that one of the skeletons was a man who apparently died from a spear wound to his back near his spine. When he was uncovered by the researchers, the white-quartz spear head was still in place.

Excavations by the archeological research team proceeded for a total of approximately ten months and to a depth of about 43 feet. Dating techniques estimated that at this depth the artifacts dated back to about 7000 B.C. which was 4000 years before the pyramids were built in Egypt. The top level artifacts indicated a discontinuance of occupancy at about the time of Columbus (around 1500 B.C.) for some unknown reason. The period from 7000 to 500 B.C. is referred to as the Archaic Period, and the period from 500 B.C. to 1500 A.D. is called the Woodland Period in the history of Native Americans. Therefore, the cave was used for a total of about 8500 years, and later excavations in the early 1960's confirmed that conclusion. Likely throughout that time the population varied considerably, but it is almost certain that there were times when relatively heavy populations were present.

The lower level of the cave is a stream passage that obviously was the source of water for the inhabitants. Now it is used by cavers who wish to explore the cave interior.

As one traverses the modern wooden walkway to the upper level just before reaching the cave there is a huge burial mound. The mound is so large it most certainly was used for interment for many years during the period of cave occupancy. Of course this raises the question of why there are some burials that were done within the cave itself presumably beneath the floor where habitation continued. However, all of the excavated human remains were dated as being from the Archaic Period when the burials were likely much less sophisticated than those of the later period.

The cave with the surrounding area including the burial mound was established as a National Monument in 1961 by proclamation of then President John F. Kennedy.

At the back of the occupied portion of the upper level is a number of very large limestone blocks. By best estimate these blocks fell from the ceiling about 3000 years ago. If the assumptions about population levels in the cave are accurate, this breakdown of the ceiling at that time may have resulted in a number of deaths. However, due to the difficulty and hazards of excavating under rubble of those dimensions, this has not been confirmed.

Our paranormal investigation team was met at the administration building on a warm June evening by several Park Rangers who had chosen to be there well beyond their normal work hours to greet and escort us on the hunt. Ten members of our AFFPR Team were able to attend, so a wide variety of equipment was available: video cameras, digital cameras, digital and tape recorders, night vision scopes, thermal scanners, and EMF detectors.

One of the Park Rangers took a reconnaissance trip up the wooden walkway to the cave to chase any snakes who might have decided to camp on the walkway for the evening. Having done that, he and the remaining Rangers escorted our Team up past the burial mound into the cave entrance. The walkway takes a short circular loop only a few feet into the cave. However, from the walkway one can view the entire portion of the cave that had been occupied in prehistoric times. A few Native American mannequins and a fake fire had been placed for effect within the viewing area in front of the breakdown.

We had heard that some paranormal activity had been reported there, but we really had no idea what to expect. Activity of this sort is often reported in areas known to have been inhabited by Native Americans. In fact psychics and other "sensitives" tend to avoid such sites. But we felt safe enough with the large assemblage of ghost hunters and Park Rangers.

Almost immediately upon arrival inside the cave, digital cameras began flashing. And almost immediately the cameras began picking up small bright lights and transparent spirit orbs that were not in the visible wavelength range of our eyes. They were certainly showing up on the viewing screens though. They tended to blink in and out and float around. Some of the Rangers who had never witnessed a spectacle such as this were photographing the orbs along with the rest of us. One important observation was that the majority of the activity seemed to be in front of the large breakdown boulders. This would tend to support the theory that sudden, traumatic deaths occurred there.

The recorders both of the digital and the tape variety were started and pointed toward the back of the cave where the ghostly activity was occurring. We would run these for a period of time, shut them off, move them to a different location, and restart them. If we were lucky enough to record any voices from the past, we wouldn't know until reviewing the recordings later. Likewise, the video recordings would be reviewed later hopefully to contain footage showing that which was unseen by us.

After about 30 minutes within the cave the Rangers led us out to the burial mound, and along the way a small blue light was seen beside the path. Photographing from the viewing area toward the mound, an uncountable number of orbs were captured. Some remaining stationary allowing their photos to be made, and others moving rapidly as supercharged orbs across the camera's field of vision.

Each of us had started a voice recorder within the cave while we were visiting the burial mound and left them there in the quiet darkness. After another thirty minutes we returned to the cave interior to retrieve the recorders and to continue photographing. At this time one of the Team members captured in the viewing screen of his digital camera an ominous red ectoplasm. There are some who believe that when these entities appear red they tend to be angry and often malevolent.

In all the investigation lasted for about two and one-half hours, but it only took the first few minutes to confirm what we had heard. The cave is most certainly haunted with the spirits of prehistoric Native Americans.

The greatest surprises, however, awaited us. Over the next couple of days the recordings were reviewed. Two separate EVP's had been captured. One was an indiscernible young female voice, and the other was a very spooky, somewhat musical chant that sounds like several voices in harmony. Perhaps there was a shamanic ritual in progress, and we happened to capture a couple of seconds of these voices from the distant past.

Over the course of 8500 years surely many thousands of individuals lived in and around this most perfect of shelters. It remained at a relatively constant temperature, so it seemed cool in the summer and warm in the winter. Food (both plants and animals) was plentiful in the forests that reached right up to the cave itself. And water was there within easy reach. The hardy individuals of prehistory lived, hunted and fished for food, gathered plants for food and medicines, made weapons and tools, worshipped their gods, and passed to the spirit world all in the vicinity of this cave. After our investigation there on that warm night in June, there is no doubt in our minds or in the minds of the Rangers who accompanied us that some of those who passed on are still there not just as skeletal remains.

08/10/2002

A Witch in Tennessee?

Andrew Jackson had an encounter with the Bell Witch of Tennessee and afterwards was quoted to have said "By Gaw! I'd rather fight the entire British Army than to deal with this torment they call the Bell Witch!" Indeed Kate as the witch came to be known haunted and tormented the John Bell family during the early 1800's as the most malevolent, notorious, and widely documented haunting ever in this country.

The haunting has been described in detail in *Authenticated History of the Bell Witch and Other Stories of the World's Greatest Unexplained Phenomenon* by M.V. Ingram published in 1894 and *The Bell Witch of Tennessee* by Charles Bailey Bell and Harriet Parks Miller published in 1934. Later publications have been produced that rehash the history presented in the earlier works and add latter-day events that mostly occurred in the Bell Witch Cave which is located on the original Bell estate.

In 1807 John Bell uprooted and moved his family from North Carolina to a 1000-acre tract of land on the Red River in northern middle Tennessee. John was a well-to-do farmer who provided quite well for his family. One day he spotted an odd-looking animal in

51

one of his fields and took a shot at it. The shot missed, and coincidence or not the haunting seems to have begun at that point. It started with a tapping and scratching on the exterior walls of their two-story home. This was an innocent-enough haunting, but it was persistent progressing to the inside where it manifested itself as gnawing sounds on the bed posts. A local preacher was brought in to investigate (an early version of an AFFPR member?). When the noises began on that occasion, he tried to entice the spirit to communicate with him. He asked questions with numerical answers, and the spirit would answer by tapping out the correct number. Verbal communication ensued, beginning as a whisper which was mostly unintelligible. Over time the voice strengthened to one that was both intelligible and intelligent.

Many times the spirit was asked who she was and from where she came (the spirit was only assumed to be female). The answers were either ambiguous or later proved to be false. The purpose for the haunting, however, was never ambiguous. She declared that she was here to see John Bell to his grave and to prevent the marriage of his daughter, Betsy, to Joshua Gardner.

The haunting was continuous from 1817 to 1821. During that time hundreds of people were witness to the Witch's antics. Also, during that time the Witch was successful in both of her objectives. John Bell was found unconscious on December 19, 1820 and died the next day of an apparent poisoning. The Witch gleefully assumed full responsibility for having performed this heinous act. Betsy Bell out of fear for the consequences promised if she married Joshua broke off the relationship. After these acts the haunting took on a less sinister attitude.

In 1821 the Witch announced that she would leave but would return in seven years. As one might surmise there was considerable consternation among the members of the Bell family when the year 1828 came around. However, the Witch stayed for only about two weeks meeting with John Bell, Jr. nightly. She took this opportunity to make a number of significant predictions. She accurately predicted three major military conflicts: The American Civil War, World War I, and World War II.

At the end of the two-week period she once again announced that she was leaving but vowed to return in 107 years when all of the original John Bell family members would have passed away. In 1935, as before, there was a great deal of concern among the Bell descendants about what would happen this time. Nothing did, but many believe that this point marked the beginning of the haunting of the Bell Witch Cave which is a small cave near

Adams, Tennessee about 70 feet up the bluff of the Red River.

The paranormal phenomena in and around this cave and on the original John Bell property are many and varied. Apparitions, lights, and orbs have all been photographed in the vicinity of the cave. Physical contact with an unseen entity has been frequently reported. Being touched and/or pushed is common. On one occasion a tourist was slapped hard enough to cause her to fall backward onto the cave floor. This incident followed a rather exuberant pronouncement that the Bell Witch must be a hoax since she had not made an appearance during the tour. The recipient of this stern reproach was taken out of the cave into the sunlight where red hand and finger prints were clearly visible on her cheek.

A large orb was once photographed during a cave tour. The photograph was authenticated as being real and reputedly was sold to the media for $500. Other more mysterious photographs have in taken in and around the cave that show ectoplasm and apparitions. One picture of ectoplasm was taken at a sink hole that feeds the cave's stream. With only minimal imagination the shape appears to be that of a witch's face. One other picture worthy of note is that of a young lady, perhaps teenaged, sitting on a small flowstone within the cave. To her right and slightly behind her sitting on the flowstone with her is a male apparition with clear facial color and features. His arms encircle her but are opaque white. No one was visible with her when the picture was taken. Stories of the antics of the present-day spirit that inhabits the Bell Witch Cave and environs have been documented in several books: *Season of the Witch, the Haunted History of the Bell Witch of Tennessee* by Troy Taylor and *The Infamous Bell Witch of Tennessee* by Charles Edwin Price as well as a few others.

The cave contains a stream passage that makes it inaccessible during the rainier months of the year. It is open to the public for a fee starting in May and ending in October with special Halloween tours each year. The normal daily tours include a short history of the notorious haunting of the Bell family and some of the more recent happenings on the property. The original Bell homestead was demolished and never rebuilt. No access is permitted to the original property which includes the family cemetery with the promise that trespassers will be prosecuted.

The tours of the cave begin with a three-hundred foot trek down the hill and along the Red River bluff to the entrance. The cave is typical of the limestone solutional caves that are prevalent in this part of the country due to the extensive limestone deposits that are at or just below the surface. The stream flowing through it is at a trickle during the summer months except during times of heavy downpours. Just inside the entrance an iron-bar gate has been installed to prevent trespassing. The interior of the cave is rather nondescript. The only significant formations along the commercial trail is a small amount of flowstone, some interesting ceiling designs caused by uneven limestone dissolution, and a large stalactite at the end named the "Eagle" due to its appearance as a large bird perched with folded wings.

Flowstone within the cave

The trail is only about 100 feet long, but the cave obviously extends beyond the stopping point of the tour. To negotiate the cave any further would require traditional caving gear including hard hats, knee pads, lights, etc.

In the course of the tour the visitors are warned not to remove anything including small rocks from the cave. Bad luck befalls everyone who attempts to pilfer even a small souvenir. This is reminiscent of the lava rocks in Hawaii which when pilfered from a volcanic site bring bad luck to the thief. Nearly every day, the guide says, they receive rocks in the mail from those who did not believe what they were told. These rocks are often accompanied by letters of apology sometimes written to the Bell Witch herself. A returned rock is evidence that another former nonbeliever has been converted.

While taking the cave tour listening to the history of one of the most extreme hauntings ever to be documented and knowing the types of encounters that have happened within these limestone walls, it is easy to imagine a malevolent spirit around every corner. The Bell Witch informed John Bell, Jr. that she had been around for a million years. Will she still be around this cave for another million always updating her bag of tricks for each new generation?

HAUNTED HOUSES

08/08/2002

Unwanted Guests

The signs that indicate that a house is haunted are many and varied. For instance lights turning on and off, doors opening and shutting, footsteps in the hallways, and items being moved or disappearing are all strong indications of a haunting. Often the haunting has nothing to do with the house or its history. Sometimes the haunting traces to beyond the erection of the building itself to the land that the house or building is sitting on. Some good examples of hauntings come as a result of houses being built on top of old graveyards, battlefields, or Native American burial sites.

61

Unless you can trace the history of the place, you may never be able to ascertain why the house is haunted.

This investigation took us to the small community of Ardmore, Alabama. A family moved a mobile home behind their parent's house just over three years ago. Outwardly everything about it appeared to be as normal and unobtrusive as any other similar home in the area. However, they were soon to begin experiencing some very strange happenings that made their home something other than normal. The couple had been married for a only a few years and had two children under the age of five. The couple's young girl spent a lot of time in her bedroom. Over time this young family began noticing something very unusual about their daughter's room.

It is very normal for children of a young age to have vivid imaginations. Most of the time we chalk up unusual things that they say as part of those wonderful imaginations, and we do not give it much thought. When the parent's of this child heard their daughter talking to someone in her room naturally they asked her who it was. She said "a friend." Later that day she was overheard arguing with someone, so the father went back into her room to find out what was wrong. The little girl said that Hinga was being mean to her. The father asked her what she was talking about, and the little girl asked him why he didn't see them. The little girl went on to tell of her friends Hinga, Carmichael, and their father, Ernie. What really got his attention was that these were no ordinary names that a little girl would ordinarily come up with by herself. By the way she described them and pronounced their names one would even conclude that they were German. She went on to tell her father that they came from the hole in her closet. Upon investigation he found that there was a golf-ball sized hole in the corner of her closet.

Curious about what their daughter was going through they set up a recorder as we of the AFFPR had recommended. It recorded the little girl's conversations throughout the day. When the tape ran out, they listened to it with anticipation. Throughout the tape they could hear their daughter talking to someone in the room, but they never heard anyone reply. They were nearly convinced that she was imagining things until they got a response on the tape that would change their minds. Halfway through the tape they heard a little girl singing a song, but to their amazement it wasn't their little girl. On the tape in a little girl's voice was someone singing a song with the words "LIKE A ZOMBIE." When the parents asked their daughter about this, she told them it was Hinga that was singing.

This was only the beginning, and the AFFPR was asked to come to investigate the goings-on at their house. When we investigate private homes like this, we only take a couple of members along to avoid overwhelming the residents with so much activity. When we arrived at this house it looked very ordinary, and inside nothing seemed to be out of the ordinary. It did not take long for us to determine which room was the little girl's. There was an energy that was being exuded by this room. Although it was obviously a girl's room, just by looking we could tell nothing about what else occupied the room. It was dark when we first viewed it, but on hand we had our digital cameras, thermal meters, night vision scopes, and 35 millimeter cameras.

We walked into the room and turned on the light to get familiar with our surroundings and to survey it. We found what one normally finds in a little girl's room. The items there ranged from coloring books and dolls to bouncy balls, and so on. After we got comfortable with our surroundings, we decided to turn off the lights. We took a few pictures of the room, but we were not seeing anything. Just as we were about to call it quits, we got some activity.

Looking through the night vision scope we could see something moving in a circular motion on the back of the closet wall. Looking closer we discovered it to be a black orb. As one might imagine in the spirit realm it is believed that a black entity is of an evil or negative nature. We remembered how the little girl had talked about Ernie, the father, being mean to the kids. To confirm what we saw through the scope we took some pictures of the location, and, sure enough, it was orb activity. The strange thing about this particular orb was that it was also visible with the unaided eye. There were also detectable temperature deviations on that particular spot of the closet compared to the rest of the closet and the room.

Little girl's closet where the paranormal events originate

As the dark orb continued its motion, it was joined by another one. However, this one was a different color. It was white, which is thought to be a good or positive entity. It appeared as if they were playing chase on the back wall of the closet. We continued to get photos and watch their movements on the wall.

After about five minutes of this activity they disappeared in the direction of the hole. We wrapped up our observation and sat down with the family to share with them what we had just experienced. They also shared more stories with us.

The father told stories of late night encounters he had when everyone else was asleep. One night while he was getting something to drink from the refrigerator, he felt something go up the back of his shirt and hit him on the back of his head. He could feel where the slap had moved his hair. He turned around to see who was there, but no one was around. As he made his way back to the bedroom, he could hear footsteps following him, so as anyone would do under those circumstances he turned around to see who it might be. No one was there.

With a little bit of fear and shock in him from what happened, he returned to his bed to try to get some sleep. After about ten minutes or so lying there, he had yet another unexplained event to occur. His daughter being too terrified to sleep in her own room was sleeping on the floor beside their bed. He had dozed off for a minute or so when he awoke and realized that his little girl was on the bed staring into his face. On impulse not realizing what he was doing and after the experience he just had at the refrigerator, he knocked her off the bed. When he did realize what had happened, he called her name to see if she was ok but got no answer. She stood up slowly and walked stiff-legged back to her pallet on the floor, laid down, and went right back to sleep. The next morning when they awoke he asked her if she was ok, but she did not remember anything that had taken place.

Other out-of-the-ordinary events have taken place quite often. While cleaning the little girl's room, the mother has also had some unnerving experiences. On occasion she would pick up the toys from the floor and place them in the toy box only to find them back on the floor when she turned back around. That was a strong indicator that it was a child that was playing tricks on her. Toys that would make musical sounds started playing spontaneously, and upon picking them up they would stop. As soon as she laid them down again, they would start playing.

The little girl who often sees and plays with the visitors

Certainly if you have the right program on television, a child will be entertained for a very long time, but if the program is changed to adult-style entertainment or news programs, you lose them immediately. On several occasions the family experienced their television acting very strange. Sometimes the channels would change from the news to a cartoon channel on its own. When the channel was changed back to the news, the same thing would happen again. If the channel was again changed to the adult program, the television would turn off by itself. Often times the volume would also vary. It would turn down to a very low volume almost if someone was trying not to make a lot of noise. Other times the volume would turn to high as if someone needed to hear it at a distance.

The little girl of the family had a remote control car in her bedroom that had not been working for a few months. One night while watching television, the family heard a very unusual noise coming from the bedroom. Straining to figure out what could make such a noise, they looked, and down the hall the remote-controlled car came rolling right into the living room. Astounded they waited to see what would happen next. The car sat there as if it had been pushed all the way from the bedroom. If it had just been pushed in the bedroom, it would have long stopped before covering the full fifteen feet of the distance to the living room. Besides they had heard the sound of the car, and it sounded like it was being controlled by the remote. The father walked over to the stopped car and noted something very strange. There was no back on the car, and there were no batteries in it.

The little girl would tell her parents that the man, Ernie, was mean. She said that Ernie was the children's father, but he wasn't a very nice man at all. Many times when Ernie would appear the kids would run and hide and sometimes completely disappear. She described him as a tall man with a beard and dark hair. She also said that he talked very funny. She described all of them to us down to the clothes they wore. From her description

69

and from their names, we began to do the research. Names being the only clues that we had, we determined the most common use of the names as that of German origin.

Our most puzzling question was why they were there. The home was not old, and no one had ever died in it. So next we tried to trace the property. This was extremely difficult because there were no historical markers to guide us. The land had been in the family for as long as anyone could remember. So tracing the property to obtain a line on the origin of these spirits was not successful.

We often wonder why these visitors are here. What is their purpose? Were they just passing through the small town of Ardmore when suddenly their lives were taken? Maybe the house is on a haunted plot of land, or maybe there are some certain artifacts in the house that carry the remains of these particular ghosts. Why is it that only the little girl is able to actually see them?

Children accept what they see and do so until they are taught different. As they begin to grow up most are taught that ghosts and spirits do not really exist. Therefore, over a period of time they begin to view these phenomena as if their minds are playing tricks on them. What if everyone still had the open mind of a child so that they accepted what they see? The reporting of apparitions would surely be much more common. This family that we saw has accepted the fact that they do not live alone, and that these unwanted guests have made their house a home.

The Queen Still Reigns

The J.W. and Itura Colley Family built their home in Grantville, Georgia in 1896 to resemble a castle. Members of this wealthy and prominent family who were very active in both politics and art throughout their history lived in the home until 1981. The Colleys founded the textile mills in Grantville, and in addition were prosperous farmers and bankers. Famous guests to the beautiful mansion included such notables as Franklin D. Roosevelt who from time to time stopped here on his way to Warm Springs, Georgia.

The Colley's son, Stewart, and his wife, Mary, and his family lived in the house now known as Bonnie Castle during and after World War II. Mary's passions were the Methodist Church and the Democratic Party in that order. One bedroom in the castle was named the Prophet's Chamber, in honor of the many clergymen who visited the Colleys. In a time when few women held positions of political power, Mary Colley served on the platform committee for Franklin D. Roosevelt. As a result of her political activities, many special visitors stayed at Bonnie Castle, including Ellis Arnall, Jimmy Carter, and Madame Chiang Kai-Shek.

The present owners of the mansion, the Palmers, moved into it in 1992. At that time they didn't know it was haunted, but even if they had known, they probably would have bought it and opened a bed and breakfast anyway. "They've never bothered any of our guests," said Patti Palmer, referring to the ghostly visitors. "Whoever they are, they are just curious. They want to make sure whatever we're doing with the house is ok." They opened the castle as a bed and breakfast about a year after they moved in. In only a few days they had the first indication that the house had a ghost. "We heard something break in the middle of the night, a big crash," Mrs. Palmer said. "We didn't know what it was, but we decided it would still be broken in the morning, so we went back to sleep. The next morning we looked everywhere: the basement, the attic, everywhere, but we couldn't find a thing that was out of place. It was strange." Soon, the Palmers also began noticing a "musty smell" from time to time, which seemed to coincide with a feeling that something or someone was there. "At one point," Mrs. Palmer said, "I went into one of the rooms, and although the windows were open, I smelled that musty smell in just a small space. When I said 'Is there anything I can help you with?' the smell immediately went away."

Only one person, the three year old daughter of one of Mrs. Palmer's friends, has reportedly seen the ghost. The little girl was sitting on the steps of Bonnie Castle eating blueberries when she started waving and calling for someone to come in the gate. She was normally a quiet child, so naturally her mother went to find out why she was so excited. She waved and ran to the front gate asking someone to come in to play with her. Her mother, not seeing anything, asked her what this person looked like. She said it was a man wearing a yellow shirt, straps, and a hat. The adults saw no one. After a few minutes the child lost interest. There is a photograph found in the attic of Mr. Colley (the original owner of the house who died in 1898) wearing a light color shirt, suspenders, and a garden hat.[3]

---

[3] Information obtained with the help of Mr. & Mrs. Palmer – the Present owners and Innkeepers of Bonnie Castle

One of the members of the AFFPR decided this was an ideal place to spend his honeymoon. He and his new bride had really wanted to spend the night in a castle so here was one in the South only a few hundred miles from home. How convenient! Fantasy for them both had now become a reality. The remainder of this story is told from their perspective.

Upon arriving at Bonnie Castle it was amazingly clear that this was no regular house. Once we ventured inside this enormous three-story house it simply took our breath away. We were lucky enough to be able to get the biggest suite there, and this proved to be a great choice. Because we could hear all the noises in the house from squeaky floors, creaking doors, and footsteps on the stairs, the first night was restless. We just thought that the house was settling due to its old age.

The second night we had the entire castle to ourselves with the exception of only the innkeepers who stayed on the first floor in the maid's chambers. They made us well aware that if we needed them, we would have to knock loudly on their door because the walls were made with twelve inches of solid wood. They also told us that since no one else would be spending the night, we were free to investigate the whole castle as we pleased. Taking advantage of the offer, we decided to do just that. We searched each room with anticipation. The feeling of someone present or someone following us was very strong. This feeling was very strong in one of the rooms where a prayer bench used to be. The original owner would invite ministers to stay in this room, and she would do her best to try to scare them. She made manikins in her spare time, would have them made up to resemble a corpse, and lay them in the minister's bed before they arrived. One can imagine how they reacted to this.

Long after the original owner passed away, many visitors have reported feeling someone's hand on them as they would kneel to pray. We did not experience this, but we sure felt as if someone was watching over us as we moved about doing our investigation. We took a few photographs with the digital camera before something started tinkering with the electronics. The innkeepers had warned us that the ghost was a prankster who would often toy around with anything that had to do with electricity. We had put a new set of batteries in the camera only to discover they had drained after five pictures. So respecting the ghost's obvious wishes, we decided that we would not reload to take more pictures that night. We decided to head back to our room so that we could review the few pictures that we were able to get and to try to obtain some EVP's. While reviewing our pictures, we discovered that someone had walked the halls with us. There was an old black and white dress on a display mannequin in one of the hallways, and where the neck and head is supposed to be, we photographed a very bright orb. This dress was definitely one that was from a different era and it appeared that maybe someone from that earlier time was trying it on.

07/28/2002

The dress to the left has a bright orb at the neckline

After reviewing the pictures and discussing the orbs that we had photographed, we decided to start our recording session. We started by asking questions such as: "What year is it?" "What is your name?" "How old are you?" "Are you in any pain?" Then we made the statement: "If there is anyone here, please let your presence be known on this recording." We often use a wide range of questions, and this helps get an EVP. We give the ghost or spirit several different opportunities to communicate with us during the session. This

77

method lets us know if the EVP is an imprint or if the spirit is being interactive. After about ten minutes of recording, we reviewed what we had to see if we had made a connection. We listened to the first four minutes or so and thought that we had been unsuccessful. However when the statement was made "If there is anyone here, please let your presence be known on this recording," a loud screech-type yell came over the recorder. We were expecting the communication from the spirit to be normal speech as we had experienced in so many investigations before, but that didn't happen this time. After reviewing the pictures once more and playing back the recording, we decided to call it a night.

We got ready for bed and decided to listen to the radio. The radio was a small, alarm-clock type that was located next to the bed on a little table that served as a night stand. After about ten minutes of talking and listening to the radio, the ghost obviously decided that he or she didn't like what we were listening to because it suddenly went silent. We thought the station had gone off the air, but we discovered that someone had turned the volume control all the way down. Mrs. Palmer, the inn keeper, had told us of a similar instance when someone who had stayed in that room had awakened one night to discover that someone had turned on the same radio and that time had turned the volume up all the way. We continued to have this happen throughout our stay there. In retrospect we should have tried a number of different types of music to try to determine what type the ghost preferred.

The next morning we went down for breakfast, and the inn keepers were curious to hear if we had discovered anything during our investigation. As we began to tell them, they would look at each other and knowingly smile. Since they knew how interested we were in the paranormal, Mrs. Palmer shared a couple of their own personal experiences with us. She told of how many times various people had seen a ghost cat walking on the second floor. Ghost animals are not as uncommon as one might think. She told us of her husband's first encounter with the ghost while he was on the second floor of the castle removing a heater in one of the rooms. He was trying to unbolt the heater and remove it from the floor when he felt someone leaning over his shoulder. He thought it was his wife so he asked her kindly to back up. He continued to feel her over his back. He asked her three times and then became a little frustrated. At that point he felt someone put their hands on his shoulders, so he turned around only to discover no one was there.

Next we decided to visit a local cemetery that was only about four minutes from the castle. We were amazed by the enormous size of the tombstones there. Many stood at least four foot tall and probably weighed in excess of four hundred pounds. There was a small road that made its way through the cemetery. We drove to find the burial site for the Colley's. We were in luck. We managed to find the location where the whole family had been buried. We were amazed to find so many from the family that close to the castle. Nightfall was upon us by now so we decided to take a couple of pictures and run the recorder. The cemetery was very active that night as our pictures proved that the Colley's were still there lingering about. The best picture we got there had four very bright and solid orbs in the Colley family burial plot.

About thirty minutes later we made our way back to the castle. On the way back, we listened to the recording to see if we had captured anything. We had gone through the same questions that we had done the night before inside the castle, and we obtained the same response. The high-pitched scream or screech came through loud and clear once more after the statement "If anyone is here, please let your presence be known on this recording."

07/30/2002

The four bright orbs at the Colley burial site

Time had quickly slipped away from us that night, and it had already gotten late so we retired in preparation for the next day. Nothing happened until the point where we would try to get to sleep. At that time we heard footsteps walking up the stairs, across the floor, and someone pushing on our door. We knew it couldn't have been the innkeepers because the foot steps would never be heard going back down the stairs.

The next morning we sat down at the table to eat breakfast and to share last night's experiences with the innkeepers. We told about the pictures and the recordings that we had gotten. They were amazed by how much activity we had experienced at the castle and

81

the graveyard. She shared a picture with us that morning that was very interesting. It was a picture of her daughter's wedding. Her daughter was married in the castle, and in one of the pictures showing her holding hands with the groom a very large orb was covering their hands. They believe that the orb is one of the Colleys saying that they approve of the marriage and that their blessing is upon it.

We changed into some comfortable clothes to sit on the porch and enjoy the perfect summer weather. One of us finished before the other and went down to talk to the innkeepers. The other stayed behind to finish getting dressed for the day. Here it was broad daylight and the ghost decided to begin its pranks again. As had happened a few nights before, the volume of the radio would go up and down and the stations would suddenly change at will. Footsteps were heard coming up to the door and then suddenly stopping not to be heard walking away. At one point one of the doors from another room opened and closed very suddenly, but no one was there.

Who knows whether the castle is haunted because it is so close to the cemetery, or whether the cemetery is haunted because it is so close to the castle. Maybe it is that whoever is haunting the castle makes his or her return to the graveyard to visit the rest of the family on a regular basis. If you ask those who are familiar with this castle, they will tell you that it is haunted by one of the Colley's nicknamed Love. Maybe love for the castle is the main reason for the frequent visits made by Love. Who knows why she is still here? Maybe she feels that she still belongs in the castle. Maybe she is afraid that someone is going to destroy the dreams that it took her family so many years to build. Whatever the reason may be, we walked away believing that a very strong presence still remains in this castle fit for a "Lovely" Queen.

Caveat Emptor!

As has been mentioned previously one of the most puzzling situations we face in some of our investigations is the lack of historical perspective we are provided about the subject site. This almost always happens when someone moves into a house or buys one that is very old, and they have little or no contact with the original or previous owners. Often people end up selling their property because it is haunted and needless to say they never even let the buyers know the situation. Caveat emptor! Let the buyer beware!

In the case we are about to describe the history is sketchy with no real indication of the source of the haunting. The house was built in the 1940's in rural Marshall County, Alabama. The builder lived in the house for more than 30 years. During that time he was the victim of a nasty robbery. He was tied to a chair on his back porch and beaten severely, but he survived. Afterwards he moved to Florida where he lived until he passed away without ever returning to Alabama. The property changed hands five times over about a twenty-year span until the present owners took possession in 1998. Very little is known about the five intervening families. However, it is quite certain that the house was haunted prior to 1995. The couple who took possession that year reported seeing a little girl walking about the house and shadow people on numerous occasions.

The present owners of the house had no idea what they were getting into when they bought the property. From the outside appearance one would consider it to be a typical farmhouse. However, the family that lives there will tell you there is nothing normal about the goings-on they experience on a daily basis inside their home. A local legend they have heard is that there was a dispute about money that is supposedly buried on the land the house is on or somewhere near by. They have thought that perhaps that the ghostly presence in their house is searching for that money.

We were flabbergasted by the myriad of stories the family shared during our initial interview with them. They did not know who or what was haunting their home but no doubt something was there that should not have been. The wife told us of the shadows she had often seen in the different rooms of the house. She said that no matter where she went, she always had an uneasy feeling that someone was watching and following her. She had this feeling all around the house, and it is very difficult for her to be alone in any room by herself for any significant period of time.

There is a room with a closet off her bedroom that was made by enclosing an area that was the back porch where the original owner was tied and beaten. She does not even consider going into this room and is uneasy just having the door open. She uses the room for storage so when she had to put something into the room she would open the door and slide the object in with her foot.

A preteen daughter in the family has had some very interesting experiences of her own in her room which is located in the back corner of the house. At times she would be lying in bed only to feel an unseen presence sit down beside her. After a time this entity would begin to stroke and gently tug her hair. One night she awoke to the bed covers being pulled under her bed. Thinking it was the family dog, she looked to discover that he was not there. She has seen black shadows materialize and move about the room to ultimately disappear into the ceiling. As if these things were not enough, she also has had the feeling of extreme coldness surround her and sometimes to follow her when she leaves the room.

The daughter told her mom that someone had been knocking the television remote control off the table. Her mother did not really believe it until she had experienced it for herself. One morning she was on the couch waiting for the time to start getting the kids ready for school when she hear a noise of sometime falling onto the floor. She looked to see the remote control on the floor beside the couch. She went to see if the daughter had done it, but she was still asleep in her bed.

There is a long list of paranormal events reported by the different members of this family within their house:

- Items being missing and mysteriously returning
- Light bulbs blowing after very short life spans
- New batteries being drained suddenly
- The sound of items falling in the attic and in the tool room that later investigation revealed nothing had happened
- The dog reacting as if there are unseen presences in the room with him
- A slapping sound in midair near the dog followed by him yelping in pain
- The dog has been eating dog treats that he wasn't given by any family member
- The feeling of being watched
- Shadow people seen daily floating about waist high through the dining room or bed room
- The sound of footsteps
- The sound of whispery voices
- Cold spots

- The apparition of a little girl with blond hair in a white dress sitting on the couch
- Numerous photographs of orbs, shadows and vortexes

Vortex photographed in front of the back room

As one might imagine this was an ideal site for a team of paranormal investigators. With each new piece of information that the family shared with us, our anticipation grew.

We arrived and after the usual introductions split up to allow a couple of people to check each room. Our first sign of activity came with orbs showing up on the digital cameras throughout the house. We set up a video camera in the bedroom in front of the closet in order to see if we could get a response as we opened the door. As soon as the door was opened, orbs were clearly visible on the video screen. They continuously made circular motions around the investigation-team members. One of the strangest orbs that we saw that night came after one of our members looked into the closet. She opened the door to see if she could photograph something paranormal there but had no success. As soon as she turned her back to walk away an orb flew across the wall and followed her out the door. It was as if someone hid, watched her, and waited for her to turn her back so they could sneak by.

During the night we had the digital voice recorders running most of the time. Due to lack of time while at the location, we decided to wait to review the recordings away from the house. We didn't want to keep the family up too late reviewing all these recordings, and we wanted to be able to review them in a quiet place in case some EVP's were low or whispery. What we recorded that night was unbelievable. We discovered there were as at least two ghosts present: a young girl and a man. As we made our way through the rooms the little girl had apparently been following us probably out of curiosity as to what we were doing there. Not only had she been following us, but she also had been talking to us. We did not hear it while we were there, but throughout the recording there was a plea for help. At first we could not believe our ears but as we listened more and more closely, we could hear a little girl's voice saying "HELP ME" a number of times.

We also had recorded (not heard) a man's voice. From the sound of the raspy voice it seemed that he was probably over forty and a smoker. We recorded him when we set up the video camera in front of the closet door in the bedroom and opened it. It sounds as if the man is searching for someone in order to get revenge for an unknown reason. On the recording the man said "PAYIN' EM BACK." Did someone wrong him in life, and was he on a mission to find them and pay them back for their misdeed.

After reviewing our information and contacting the family, they were very eager to have us come back. Immediately after we had left they took more pictures. On them they had captured even more paranormal activity throughout the house.

They believed that the ghosts knew when we were coming back for another investigation, and activity started to increase several days before we got there. We loaded up and made the drive to this little house in Arab once more about three weeks later. This time we took along ten members to try to obtain more information from this haunting. When we arrived, we were greeted at the door by the family. We shared with them our findings and played the EVP's from the first time we had been there. They were amazed just as we were by what we had captured and were anxious to see if we could get anything else.

Like the previous time, we split up into groups and investigated the different rooms of the house. As we had learned during the first visit, the girl's room, the bedroom, and the closet were hot spots for paranormal activity so that is where we spent most of our time. As we had been told the family had problems with the ghosts affecting anything electrical. We had the same experience almost upon arrival. The batteries in the cameras were draining very quickly. We were only able to photograph a few orbs before two of the cameras went dead so we focused mainly on audio recording.

We began a question and answer session in the girl's bedroom in an effort to elicit a communication with whoever was haunting this room and to try to get information that would help us to know what he or she was doing there. Our questions were such that one word answers would be sufficient. "How old are you? "What is your name?" "Are you in any pain?" "Are you scared?" "Do you have a message for us?" Two sessions that consisted of about 20 minutes each in her room were held, and we moved on to the main bedroom and the back room.

Two of us went into the back room to hold another question and answer session. The closet door was open and a number of items were scattered about confirming the statement that the wife had given us that she tended to push things inside the room rather than to enter it. We shut the door behind us and turned off the light, so we were surrounded by total darkness. About two minutes into our questions we received a response. The comment was made that the people in the house were afraid, and we asked if they had a reason to be. The closet door slowly closed. We stayed in the room for a few more minutes to see if anything else would happen, but it did not.

Next we set up the video camera in the same location as in the last hunt, and we again weren't disappointed. As soon as the taping started, we began to capture orbs. They were moving at a very fast speed as seen in the camera screen, but they could not be seen with the naked eye. As in the last hunt, this activity only lasted for a minute or so and then disappeared once again for the night. By this time it was getting quite late so we decided to review the rest of our photographs, recordings, and video tapings after we got home.

The next morning, before we had time to review all that we had obtained, the family contacted us once again. They told us how much activity they had experienced once we had left. They sent us a picture of a black shadowy figure that was photographed in the corner of their bedroom against the wall near the ceiling. The daughter described it as what she had seen before in her bedroom. This was also the same type of shadow that had been reported as following the mother around in the house. It was obvious to us this had to be a shadow person although it did not have a definite human-like shape.

She said after we had left they decided to go through the house and to do what we had been doing. They used the digital camera to take shots in the places that we had visited and had our question and answer sessions. During this time they were able to photograph the shadow. As she began to talk more and more about the experiences of the night before, she became very eager to learn what additional

information we had gathered. She wanted us
to let her know as soon as we could.

Shadow photographed following the second visit

After the conversation with the family,
we could not wait any longer to review our
information. What we obtained on our digital
recorders was staggering. It only took about
two minutes to get a response from the ghosts.
In much of the recording it was very close to
being an normal interview with them
considering how interactive the session was.
As soon as a question was asked, we would
get an answer. To someone who had not been
there, the recording would sound like a regular
real time interview.

In the girl's bedroom we got our first
response. A male voice said "I AM HERE."

From that point on the questions that were asked received responses in a little girl's voice. The first question was "How old are you?" The little girl answered "EIGHT." To the question "Are you in any pain?" she said "NO,. NO." When asked if she was scared, the reply came "YES." The final response came when we asked for her name. She replied "HEATHER." All of the responses were in a low whisper. Were we the ones that were scaring her?

Our next set of EVP's was recorded in the back room with the closet. The most disturbing of them came almost as soon as we turned out the light. It was an unintelligible very high-pitched scream. We first thought it to be recorder noise but ruled that idea out when it was also captured on three other recorders that were going at the time. The next recording was of the door shutting when we were in the midst of asking questions. It sounded like someone had taken the door handle and either pulled the door shut with a slam or pushed it shut from the outside. The most disturbing EVP of the night came right after the door closed. About twenty seconds later a male said in a whisper "SHAUN." This was the name one of the two people that were in the room and one of the authors of this book.

It appears that the ghosts were becoming more accustomed to us during this second visit. To have an interview session and to call one of the investigators by his first name was much more than we could have expected. It reinforces the idea that ghosts are intelligent entities that attempt to communicate with our level of existence more often than we know.

What is the relationship between the man and the little girl? What keeps them bound to this house? Are these two separate hauntings coincidentally taking place at the same time? Maybe Heather will continue to communicate with us so we can learn more about her and why she is so afraid. Maybe the man had something to do with the legend of the money? Maybe this money disturbs his rest until it is found or until someone unknown to us knows about it. Or maybe it is a family of ghosts haunting this house. As the folks living there now keep inviting us back and as communication with the ghosts grow stronger, maybe we can find the answer to our most perplexing question, "Why are you here?"

Den of Activity

It was now mid November, the rush of Halloween excitement had diminished, and our team was busy researching and prospecting for future investigations. We were contacted by some family members concerning their former family homestead. We proceeded with a phone interview and screening process, and at the conclusion set a date and time for a basic walk through of the location. There were only three of us which made the trip to the home that night. We were met there by some of the family members which had spent their childhood growing up there. The house was a normal looking average home, the kind of house you would you find in most neighborhoods throughout the nation. Nothing seemed out of the ordinary from the exterior. We greeted the family members and entered the residence. As we passed through the door's threshold there was what felt like a curtain of extreme coldness as if we had entered a giant freezer. It was the kind of cold that went straight to your bones. In the paranormal field extreme temperature changes such as this were a good indicator of a ghostly presence. We started taking temperature reading with our thermal meter right away and quickly determined that the temperature outside the house was warmer than inside.

The house had been unoccupied for sometime, and the electrical power had been disengaged for months, so as usual we proceeded with an air of expectancy. We entered and began to get some basic readings and gather some additional information from the family. One of our team members began to take some pictures of the interior of the house as I spoke with some of the family. I received a tap on my shoulder and I turned around and was shown a digital camera display with what appeared to be an orb on it. An orb has been defined by paranormal researchers to be the basic form of spirit energy. Orbs appear as round balls of light which can be captured with any type of camera. This phenomenon can show up in pictures in a wide variety of appearances such as almost completely transparent to solid. Orbs sometimes look like cells under a microscope or the round body of a jellyfish. Since orbs cannot be seen by the human eye most of the time we rely on cameras to catch them. In order to properly identify paranormal phenomenon in photographs our team has what is known as a base line of evidence. This base line is used to compare and analyze the photos and either confirm or deny their authenticity.

Once I saw the picture that had been taken, I got my camera from its case and began taking pictures. As we were taking photos we began our walkthrough of the house. Once we had taken pictures of every room of the house we packed our equipment and thanked the family for the opportunity. We advised them that we would get back in touch with them in a few days with our initial results. We then proceeded to a team member's house to review the pictures and events of the walkthrough while they were still fresh on our minds. The amount of activity in our pictures was incredible. With the level of results like this we knew a full investigation of this home would by no means be a waste of time and resources. We contacted the family and set up an over night stay for our team in the residence.

Prior to meeting at the house we scheduled a team meeting to go over the investigation plans and go over our initial results from the first visit. Once the final details were covered we set out for the house. When we arrived the family members were there already waiting parked in the driveway. One family member got out of their car and unlocked the door for us. We all entered the home this time without the freezer effect coming through the door. We then did introductions for the team members that did not attend the walk through and began to set up our equipment. We first set up our video camera on tripods to cover many different angles yet overlap for affirmation purposes.

We started rolling video tape and then proceeded to get our still cameras ready for action. It did not take long before we knew we had some unseen occupants that did not like so many guests. Some of our video cameras immediately started having power failures. Researchers have reported rapid if not immediate power loss in active paranormal locations. The theory behind this is that some ghosts pull energy from the environment in order to manifest themselves. Some theories also state that ghosts can take energy from humans and their emotions such as fear, anger, or love as well. Having been in paranormally active places many times our team was prepared with lots of backup batteries on hand. We replaced the batteries and began rolling tape once again. It was odd was that all three cameras batteries died at the same time. The team began taking photographs with our digital and 35mm cameras. We began getting orbs right out of the gate. We had a team member take a picture with a digital camera which showed what looked like a face on one of the walls. One of the family members took a look at this picture and gasped for breath in shock. "I can't believe it!" they exclaimed. "I will be right back." and they scurried out the door. They quickly returned with a picture of their deceased father which had appeared in the obituaries of the local newspaper a few years ago. The face that had appeared in the photograph looked exactly like the picture of their Dad. We were all surprised to see with our own eyes such an incredible occurrence. From that point on we knew that we were in a very active house.

Snapping pictures and rolling video tape continued in the same area where we had captured the face on the wall. Suddenly the entire group including the family experienced a rush of extremely cold air that flooded the entire area. It was as if someone had opened a door during an artic wind gust. "Does anyone smell that?" a team member asked. The room was filled with the overwhelming smell of beer. Everyone there experienced the odor as if we had just mopped the room with a bucket of beer. One of the family members stated that there dad was a beer drinker and enjoyed drinking a beer on a daily basis. The family member went on to say that when they would be close to him or hug him they would often smell beer. The entire team and family were in total agreement that the family may have been contacted by their Dad. Maybe he just wanted to let them know he was still there, and he knew they would recognize the events as having his signature on them.

We decided to investigate the remainder of the house for more paranormal phenomena. We proceeded to the bedrooms to collect data with our equipment. After a time in the bedrooms we decided to go check on the video equipment since we had experienced massive power drain previously. We had digital cameras and have gotten good results by turning quickly and snapping a picture behind us. So as we walked down the hallway to the den, but before we entered the room a camera was stuck in and a picture was taken. We paused as we waited for the camera to save the picture to its memory and pulled up the photo for a quick view. We were amazed to see what is known as a power orb or sometimes called a super charged orb. It was long comet like orb that looked a lot like a streak of orange neon that ran across the entire den just below the ceiling. At that point we began to take more pictures in hopes of getting another shot of this power orb in motion. Nothing showed up in any of the other pictures that were taken. So we decided to re-create the event by leaving for a few minutes and then returning to take another picture from the same spot with an element of surprise. We retreated for about ten minutes and then went back for another crack at catching the power orb again. We approached and snapped just as before and waited in anticipation as the camera saved the picture. When it came up there was absolutely nothing paranormal revealed in the picture.

The power orb moving close to the ceiling

The next paranormal hot spot was one of the bedrooms. Initially we got some hits on our emf detector and got a few orbs on digital cameras. On our hunts we always try something new to get a response from a ghost. This time we had the family member whose bedroom this was to sit inside along with another team member and shut the door. Then we knocked on the door and had the family members ask "Who is it?" We had video cameras rolling tape and other cameras ready to shoot. One person knocked on the bedroom door and the family member said "Who is it?" just as we had planned. An ice cold wind rushed down the hall which gave us immediate chills. The person who knocked turned the door knob but could not open the door. It was as if there was someone pressing up against the other side. He kept adding more and more force to the door until all of a sudden it released. The door flew open. We took pictures in the room which was still ice cold. The team member that was inside the room when the door was closed had knocked took a picture just as the door flew open and caught what is know as a vortex. A vortex has been defined by paranormal researchers as many balls of light or orbs which combine together. Vortexes are funnel shaped and most appear to be white in color and resemble a small tornado. Vortexes are extremely rare and this was the team's first vortex to be captured in a photograph.

As it got later and later into the night the family members decided to call it quits and turn the house over to us for the remainder of the night. We wanted to cover every inch of the

to document any other paranormal activity. We investigated the house's attic and even crawled under the floor. For the duration of the night we did not experience any more paranormal activity. It was if someone had turned off a switch. We all felt that the activity was for the purpose of possibly communicating with the family members that were present earlier that night. As the sun began to rise we packed our equipment into our cars, locked the door to the house, and departed. I spoke with the family the next day and found out that we had confirmed for them that the house was active and they were not crazy. Our entire team was grateful to have had the experience and even more satisfied to have helped someone to confirm the suspected identity of the entity residing here.

A Potpourri of Haunted Sites

The Phantoms of the Whole Backstage Theater

In the late 1960's the local thespians of the Guntersville, Marshall County, Alabama area came together to form an acting troupe that came to be known as the Whole Backstage Theater. The old Rock Schoolhouse, a former elementary school then closed, proved to be the perfect setting for such an endeavor. Centrally located within the building was the school auditorium (stage and all) which was ideal for the theater itself. Surrounding the auditorium were classrooms, and these would be put to use for housing the various needs of the theater: costume storage, prop storage, set construction materials, shop, changing rooms, etc. A few adjacent rooms on one side of the building were combined to form a small children's theater. Thus with a troupe and a home, the Whole Backstage Theater was set to begin. Since the time that the theater was established, it has been known that the old building harbors at least two denizens of a bygone era.

The entire team of paranormal investigators of the AFFPR assembled on a Saturday night for the trip to Guntersville to the Whole Backstage Theater. We arrived and were led to a conference room. Right away it became obvious that this theater preferred some of the more macabre classics such as *Arsenic and Old Lace*, *The Little Shop of*

110

Horrors, and *Phantom of the Opera* from the playbills that were posted around the room. How interesting that we were here to investigate paranormal phenomena that had been observed and to see that this type of production was done here so often!

The initial interview was to provide a brief history and to relate some of the anecdotal evidence of the haunting of the building for our team and for one member of the media. On at least two occasions a boy in the age range of 8 – 10 has been seen in one of halls on the west side of the building. On one of these occasions a gentleman who was a former teacher and who is now associated with the theater was in a hall getting a soft drink from the machine located there. While standing at the machine making a selection the boy dressed in a striped shirt and long pants appeared, walked past him with a purposeful look on his face, and disappeared at the intersection with the next hallway. On other occasions he has materialized as a misty ectoplasm and as a glowing, white, translucent apparition. Upon hearing these stories we were certainly anxious to make his acquaintance.

The gentleman who saw the full-body apparition of the little boy owns a large standard poodle who has often accompanied him to the theater. This dog is very friendly and does not shy away from anyone.

However, there is one hallway in the back of the building that the dog will not traverse. When brought in by a side entrance to this hallway and after taking only a few steps, the dog stops dead in his tracks. No amount of coaxing has been successful at making him walk the length of the hall.

Also in this part of the building some very unusual things have happened. Doors have been seen to open and close by themselves. Objects are lost and found in their original locations some time later. Whispering voices and other odd noises have been heard. The burglar alarm system sounds in the middle of the night at least once per month for no apparent reason.

Two of the most bizarre events have occurred in the costume storage room off the back hallway. Once one of the women who works at the theater entered the costume room only to have a shoe thrown at her. No one else was in the room. At another time a costume had received all the proper alterations to be a perfect fit for the actor. The next day the costume was found to be much too small. It had been re-altered with a primitive hand stitching. It is interesting to note that this room reputedly was the classroom for "the meanest teacher in the school." She taught in the early days of the school, and obviously conducted her classes with a sternness unrivaled by her peers at that time.

Since the building was obviously haunted by at least two different spirits at two different locations, the investigation team split into two separate groups to cover both areas. One group went to the back hall, and the other went to the west side hall where the little boy had been seen. As the investigation progressed, both groups wandered throughout the entire building.

The group in the back hall set up a video camera in the costume room, closed the door, and began asking questions. None of the questions were answered (as we found on our recorders later). However, almost immediately the video picked up a bright, fast-moving orb traveling at an angle from the floor to the ceiling. Shortly after that in the midst of the questioning a white shapeless form appeared which quickly changed to an amoeba-like orange glow. The video camera was removed from the costume room and set up on a tripod in the center of the hallway. It was left in this position until the thirty-minute tape was exhausted. Later review of the tape revealed two different occasions when fast-moving orbs appeared, traveled a short distance, and disappeared.

One member of the back-hall team went back into the dark costume room and closed the door. He stood in the dark with the digital recorder running for about five minutes. The tape was reviewed after returning home from the hunt. A low voice was recorded saying "WHAT IS THIS?" Perhaps a spirit from a different era was questioning the device being used for recording.

Do spirits have a need for bathroom facilities? Since this was formerly an elementary school, the bathroom fixtures were sized for little people. A quick shot with the digital camera into the Boy's Room showed an orb against the wall over the sink. Was this the little boy that had been spotted here? Another larger orb was photographed inside the children's theater floating on the stage. Both groups of investigators continued to photograph throughout the building all the way to the attic.

The group that went to investigate the hallway where the boy had been seen was able to photograph a misty ectoplasm at the corner where two hallways intersect. This was near the soft drink machine where the boy was first spotted as a full-body apparition. At this location another recording session was begun to try to obtain an EVP. During the questioning one person was standing close to the corner where the ectoplasm had been photographed when he felt cold air move slowly past at about waist level. A number of questions were asked in an effort to determine the identity of the spirit. When the question was asked "Do you like this school?" there was a pause, and an answer came back "I DO NOT!" Of course as usual the answer was not audible, but it had been captured by one of the recorders. The disturbing point of the answer is that there is an unfortunate spirit caught here where he doesn't want to be.

A second visit was made to the theater about one month later. Recorders and video cameras were set up at the intersecting hallways near the soft drink machine and left to operate without interference. After about an hour (the video tape only lasted thirty minutes of this time) the devices were retrieved for later review. The later review gave us some pleasant surprises from a paranormal investigator's point of view. The video cameras had been set up in such a manner as one pointed down one long hall, and the other pointed down the intersecting hall toward the first hall. This way anything moving along either corridor would be taped. Also a recorder had been placed on the water cooler in clear sight of both video cameras. Within the first few minutes of the equipment being left alone, and orb came from behind one of the cameras, moved along one wall toward the water cooler, slowed down just above the recorder placed there, and flew back along the opposite wall to behind the camera. Obviously the little boy was curious about this equipment, and he was taking a look at it. The videotape stopped at thirty minutes, but the digital recorder continued to run for another 25 minutes. At the fifty-minute point in the tape an adult male voice was heard as saying "IN THE BACK." Often EVP's are obtained that seem to be unrelated to the scene at hand. This appeared to be one of those, but how are we to know? There may be scenes being enacted at this theater that are being performed by unseen actors (at least most of the time).

08/09/2002

Weathered Stones and Spirits

When most people think of ghosts their minds compose an elaborate scenario of a graveyard, a full moon, and some type of horrific apparition. Although these elements combine for a thrill ride at movie theaters, the scene for modern day ghost hunters is very different. The objective is to approach the paranormal field of research with an open mind and to use scientific methods along with a broad range of equipment to pull data from the alleged haunted location. The successful investigator must have a recipe, which includes such ingredients as historical events, folklore, and the ever-popular urban legends. One of the locations in which we incorporated all of these is the Maple Hill Cemetery.

Maple Hill Cemetery is located in Huntsville, Alabama. Huntsville, a city of about 200,000, is noted for the space and defense industries located there. In fact one of its most celebrated citizens was Dr. Werner von Braun who led the United States from his office and laboratories in Huntsville in the space race from the 1950's through the 1970's. The most noted accomplishment of this effort was the landing on and safe return of a man from the Moon in July, 1969.

Settlement at the site which is now Huntsville began sometime between 1790 and 1800 when a few adventurous white settlers came to the area then occupied by the Cherokee and Chickasaw Indian tribes. John Hunt arrived on the scene in 1805 and built a two-room log cabin near the Big Spring which is now the center of town. In 1808 he made a squatter's-rights claim for the property on which his cabin was located during the first land sales for the northern Alabama area. The claim was denied, and Hunt moved on to unknown whereabouts. LeRoy Pope bought the land around the Big Spring and changed the name of the town to Twickenham in honor of the British home of Alexander Pope, the poet, whom LeRoy greatly admired. The new name was short-lived. The name of Huntsville was reinstated when the town was incorporated in 1811. The state of Alabama held its first Constitutional Convention there in

1819, and until 1820 it served as the temporary state capital.

At about that time the first person was laid to rest in the Maple Hill Cemetery. The cemetery spans over 100 acres with accesses that range from a full car-size drive to very narrow paths that were made for horse drawn buggies. The original records for this cemetery were destroyed by fire so it is very difficult to determine just how many graves are within the area. Some estimate that there is between 80,000 to well over 100,000 graves, which include such distinguished occupants as the first five governors of the state of Alabama. Maple Hill is surrounded by what looks like an ancient rock wall that stands about four feet high. Its main entrance is guarded by a huge black iron gate that stands open until sunset and then is locked. Inside there are countless mature trees, which give a visitor in the fall season a treat with their vivid array of autumn shades. The cemetery's interior boasts a seemingly endless sea of weathered headstones and mausoleums which constitute a wide variety from the most simple and plain to the elaborate. Some monuments are incredible hand-made masterpieces which most certainly began as shapeless boulders of stone.

Over the years there have been countless stories of ghosts that have a tie with Maple Hill. There are such folklore tales as that of a woman being buried sitting in her favorite rocking chair. The tale goes that whoever would knock on the crypt would hear the squeaking of her rocking chair. One of the most famous urban legends surrounding the cemetery is that of the angel of death. Those who saw the angel of death drove their cars up to a certain crypt and in the midst of their headlights would appear the angel. With such a reputation of alleged paranormal activity our team of paranormal investigators set our sights on Maple Hill.

It was mid November and the temperature was in the forties. The crisp autumn air had become much cooler and had a subtle sharpness. Winter is the best time of year for documenting paranormal activity at outside locations with cameras because there is no pollen or bugs, which could give an untrained eye the illusion of a ghostly presence showing up on film. We arrived in the late evening, quickly parked, and begin to gather our equipment. Our team began the investigation with a recording session using digital and tape recorders with super sensitive microphones in hopes of capturing an EVP. We walked along the paths with our recorders running in hopes of receiving a message from the unseen residents of Maple Hill. After the recording session had come to a close, our team began the next phase of the investigation. Ghostly phenomena have been directly connected to disturbances in electromagnetic fields. In order to detect such a disturbance an electromagnetic field detector is required. Using this piece of equipment enables the investigator to detect what would normally go unseen. Each team member was armed with an emf detector, and we began walking in a grid formation in the cemetery. Not long into the grid walk one of our team member's detector was engaged at a high level which let us know that there was a major electromagnetic disturbance occurring. The first thing the other team members began to do is rule out such things as power lines or underground utilities. When it was confirmed that there were no such man-made sources present in the area, we encircled the team member that was engaged and began to pinpoint the exact location when suddenly the field started moving. It was moving at what seemed to be an average walking speed for a person. It made several turns and curves in and around headstones. Just as it had engaged the electromagnetic field detector, the phenomenon stopped as quickly as a snap of the fingers or the blink of an eye. We started another grid walk (thinking we may have just lost the source) in hopes of picking the trail up once again. After about fifteen minutes had passed we noticed the sun was receding. Our time was limited due to increasing darkness and local laws which make it unlawful to be inside Maple Hill at night.

Half of our team continued a grid walk and the remainder of us began to set up our video and still cameras to get some parting shots before closing the investigation. As darkness descended upon us, we gathered our equipment and departed the cemetery allowing the shadows to reclaim their territory. Driving away from Maple Hill our entire team had the feeling that we all had experienced the unknown. A few days later we all assembled to compile the data pulled from the investigation. This investigation resulted in no electronic voice phenomena but there were two pictures that were taken with a high quality 35mm camera and a tripod that were unexplainable. The most impressive of these pictures showed what in paranormal research is called a power orb or sometimes referred to as a super charged orb. It looks like a streak of neon light with a ball on the end. It also resembles a skinny comet. The picture is still being studied in many areas such as feet per second the power orb was moving in relationship to the shutter speed of the camera. Whether these occurrences were spirits letting us know that they were there or if there is some other explanation, Maple Hill is a place one can go to experience the unknown.

A super-charger orb moving from left to right to a position above the tombstone in the middle

There is a park nestled in a wooded cove that lies directly behind the Maple Hill Cemetery. Due to its location and eerie atmosphere the park is known to locals as the Dead Children's Playground. The park is complete with a variety of playground equipment, a pavilion, and a baseball field. One of the legends is that late at night the ghost children of Maple Hill come out of the cemetery and play at the playground. Rumors even go so far to say that swings have been seen swinging as if there were children swinging in them. Other playground equipment has been seen in full motion without the slightest hint of a breeze. Along with the tales of the playground there is also a legend of a boy that was playing one day along the ledges of a cliff that surrounds the baseball field when

124

an unseen force pushed him to his death. Some people have reported that they have seen at night the transparent figure of a boy that dances in and out of the trees. Some have even said that they have heard a boy laughing and giggling which changes to a blood curdling scream making even the hardened skeptic change their stance on the existence of ghosts. With all this alleged paranormal activity the table was set for what seemed to be the making of a five star meal that would delight even the skeptical pallet.

Our team of paranormal investigators is passionate in their pursuit to collect evidence of life after death that will stand up to scientific scrutiny. We gained permission through the proper channels and set the date for the investigation of the Dead Children's Playground. It was a fall night, the air had that certain anticipation, and our team was ready to take on the mysteries that this playground held. The entryway to the park is very easily missed but thanks to antilock breaks we made the turn into the drive. As we traveled down the tree lined drive we saw the playground. It was a very neatly kept park as far as maintenance was concerned but due to such embellishment of the urban legends that this place marinates in there were lots of graffiti everywhere. We parked our cars quickly and began gathering our equipment. Every eye was glued to the swings looking for signs of movement. Nothing was moving, swaying, or even drifting. We began our walk down the sidewalk which leads into the play area. We then powered up our arsenal of equipment and started a pursuit of the ghost children. We used equipment such as a thermal meter with uses a laser to give us a surface temperature reading and also a night scope which operates in the infra red portion of the spectrum. After about an hour and a half without the slightest hint of paranormal activity we set up at the baseball field. It seemed to be just an ordinary baseball field but without dug outs or a defined infield. We assembled the team and started to work with our ghost detecting gear once again. Another hour and a half went by without any ghostly phenomena and without a transparent boy asking us to play catch.

Slightly disappointed we began to take down our equipment and bring this ghost hunt to a close. Our team having traveled to many paranormal hot spots realized that paranormal events are actually very rare. It's all about being in the right place at the right time. When you go bass fishing, you want to catch the record bass or at least one worthy of being mounted, but you are not even guaranteed a bite. Walking back to our cars and talking about future locations to investigate, someone said "I hear giggling." We all stopped walking and began to listen intently. It sounded like giggling and whispering of young voices. Just as our adrenaline started pumping at the prospect of audible ghost voices, several teenage girls rounded the bend of the drive and caught a glimpse of us standing there as motionless as statues. What came next was a unified scream, the girls running full speed in retreat, car doors slamming, and the squealing of car tires on the pavement. This night the ghost children of Dead Children's Playground were not at recess, but a few young ladies out for a thrill actually got the scare of their lives.

Entities of Madness

There is an abandoned insane asylum located in the Southeastern United States. Due to the sensitive nature and history of this facility we are keeping the location and identity a secret. We received information of this building and began our research into the history and alleged paranormal activity. It did not take us long to find a few urban legends that were associated with the asylum. The real shock came from researching the asylum's history of abuse and torture of inmates. Unbelievable levels of inhumane treatment that would even get an animal shelter condemned. It seemed in the beginning the asylum was known for its moral treatment of the mentally disturbed patients. It was famous for not using restraints of any kind and the staff seemed dedicated to the recovery of their patients. Over time the treatment, which was once a shining example of moral treatment, became a literal hell on earth for those inmates who were incarcerated behind its walls. After finding out the horrific past of the asylum our team knew if there was anyplace that were haunted by spirits seeking redemption for injustice, the old asylum would be one of them. We made arrangements to investigate the asylum for paranormal activity.

As we turned off the main road and started up the tree-lined drive of the asylum, our team was ready for anything, or so we thought. It was a very dark night in the middle of January but a little cold air never slowed down this team of ghost junkies. The drive leading us to the asylum was very rough, narrow, and long. After driving for what seemed like an eternity up the drive, the lights on our car finally revealed this massive structure to us. The building looked as if it were straight out of a horror movie. The front of the asylum had broken windows and was saturated with graffiti. We drove around the building and parked our cars in the back. The entire team was awestruck by the site of this intimidating structure. We gathered our equipment and started down the walk to the asylum. The first thing to come to mind is that this place is a ghost hunter's paradise. There was a sense of heaviness to this place, which gave us all a sense of remorse for those who were forced tp call this place home.

We entered the asylum through a door in the rear and began our journey into the past. According to records the building was abandoned sometime in the sixties and had no electricity or phones. There were old beds and equipment through out the building. Vandals with their destructive natures had made their past visits known as well with graffiti and holes that had been put in the walls. We continued to search for the main lobby where we had planned to set up a base of operations. We walked up two flights of stairs and made a turn heading toward the center of the building where we hoped to find a lobby. We went down a very long dark hall with inmate cells on each side. Proceeding with caution and light from only flashlights, we slowly passed by the open cells peering into each of them and viewing their contents. Some cells were painted different colors but all had peeling paint, and some of them had old beds and personal belongings still remaining. Just as the last team member walked past a cell, the huge door to it slammed with extreme force. We all jumped with surprise. The team quickly powered up our equipment and backtracked to the door. The thermal meter did not show a difference in temperature and the EMF did not get a reading of any change in the magnetic field. We began to roll videotape and started our voice recorders to document this event. A team member knocked on the door and asked, "May I come in?" To our surprise the thick wooden door started to creak and open very slowly. It was as if someone inside the cell was peeking out the crack to see who was there. Then the door began to open completely as if to let us know we could enter. The team was puzzled and our minds went in overdrive to figure out a logical explanation for the door slamming and opening by its self. One of the team members said: "If you want us to leave shut the door." Just as if to answer the question we all stood in awe as the door began to shut. It was not as if it slightly drifted shut but actually shut with purpose. The team member who had made the challenge said jokingly: "I will see you all in the car." We pushed the heavy cell door open and cautiously entered the dark cell. It was about ten feet by ten feet square with pink paint peeling from the walls. There were some items such as a tattered old white nightgown along with some blank sheets of white paper that were scattered on the floor. We spent a few minutes waiting on another incident, but when nothing happened we decided to continue our pursuit of documenting more of the unseen inmates of the asylum.

We made it to the center of the building and found the lobby. The room was very large with what appeared to be an office on one side and a staircase leading up. The team set up a base of operations in there. Once everything was situated we started executing our game plan. We divided into small teams to alternate manning the base and investigating. Team one was assigned to investigate the second floor while team two stayed at the base for logistics support. Team one geared up and made their way up the staircase to the second floor. Arriving on the second floor they were greeted by a wall which had been professionally painted yellow with red letters stating: "Welcome to the Second Floor." To the left and right were long pitch-black halls lined with cells on both sides. We decided to go to our left and with flashlights beaming walked slowly down the hall. Having traveled down the hall for about thirty yards the floor plan opened up to what appeared to be a nurse's station. Painted on the walls in this area were cartoon like characters. There were also some very old toys that were littered on the floor. Along with other indications that were present obviously we came to the conclusion that this area would have been the children's ward. Not only were asylums used for the mentally ill but also, some asylums were even used as orphanages for unwanted children in the early days. Our minds were consumed with what it must have been like for an orphaned child to grow up surrounded by an environment of insanity. One team member examined one of the toys and noticed it had wheels and rolled it across the floor. A few seconds passed, and a team member's electromagnetic field detector start alarming. This let us know that there was a disturbance in the electromagnetic field and can be a sign of a ghostly presence. The team member moved the EMF detector around in a small circle in order to locate the source location for the disturbance. The circular pattern did not help pin point the location so the detector was moved in a upward motion at which time the signal got weaker as it got higher. So the team member started slowly lowering the detector. As the detector got closer to the floor the level of disturbance that was detected increased. The team member asked us to stretch out our hands and place them in the general area of the detector. It was as if one had stuck one's hand into a bucket of ice water. At this point the detector's needle was showing the highest rating possible. It was then when a team member said it must be a child. Then the electromagnetic field started moving like it was crawling along the floor. We lost track of the field only once when it seemed to go into a wall. We continued the pursuit on the other side of the wall that appeared to be a closet. Suddenly it was gone. The detector went from being at its highest reading and alarming to dead silence. We moved quickly thinking the field had possibly started moving again. The team continued to cover the entire area with detectors as if we were mowing a lawn. After exhausting all our efforts and equipment, team one decided to retreat to base and document the interaction with what we considered the ghost of a child.

After documenting the complete experience on the second floor it was time for team two to go into action. Geared up and ready team two started the assent to the third floor. Arriving on the third floor the team started their investigation by doing a walk through of the entire floor. To cover ground quickly the team divided up and each member set out alone in a different direction. Due to the sheer size of the asylum it did not take the team members very long to feel isolated. One of the members was rounding a corner just as they received a friendly tap on their shoulder. Thinking that one of there other team members had some how doubled back, he turned around to find no one present. A quick chill ran over all of them, but the team member rapidly pulled out his camera and started taking pictures anyway. By this time the other members had finished their individual walkthrough and had noticed the flashes coming from the other end of the hall. The team gathered and concluded physical contact had actually taken place. No other equipment at this location registered a response of paranormal activity so team two proceeded to investigate more of the asylum. The team entered an area that seemed to contain isolation cells. Walking through this area they had a heavy sense of oppression and anger. One of the team members mentioned they felt a burning sensation on their face. The sensation kept intensifying, and we stopped to take look at it. As we shined a flashlight on his face it looked like the outline of a red handprint across the right cheek, as if someone had slapped him with an open hand. With the burning continuing to intensify we put the brakes on the investigation and started making our way back to base. Shortly after being back at base the burning had stopped, but it looked like the team members face was starting to swell. Being a hardcore ghost hunter, the team member insisted that the investigation continue without delay.

Team two was still at bat and decided to investigate another area of the asylum. The team proceeded to explore a hallway that led to the backside of the lobby area. The hall opened up to unveil a very large room. The room was full of old patient beds and at one end had what seemed to be a stage. The beds, which were numbered in the hundreds, made it difficult to move around so we were limited to only a small walking space. We decided to do a question and answer session in hopes of capturing an EVP. We asked such question as "What is your name?" with about a twenty-second pause between questions. During this session one of the team members stated they thought they heard a phone ring. We all listened closely in complete silence. A phone started ringing! It was an old bell-type ring that sounded like it was coming from the floor directly above us. The phone rang at least eight times before it stopped. We all waited for a couple minutes hoping to hear it ring again, but it did not. We wanted to go the location from where the sound was coming, so we went up the stairs and assembled where we heard the ring. We waited in silence for the ringing to start again. The ringing started back but this time the sound was coming from below us. It was coming from the area we had just come from. It was as if someone was playing jokes on us. We began a room-by-room search of the general area the ringing could have come from. No phone was ever found.

Outside the asylum dawn was quickly approaching and our time at the asylum was coming to a close. Did our team experience the afterlife of tormented souls? Or were these just your typical child-like prankster types? A night such as we had there would answer your question: Do ghosts really exist? However, it could also leave one with a lot more questions.

The Railroad Track Ghost of Chapel Hill

Chapel Hill is a small town about 35 miles as the crow flies south of Nashville, Tennessee on US 31. It's noted for the haunted L&N Railroad track that runs through it. Hundreds of witnesses attest to having seen "ghost lights" on the tracks, and on many occasions a ball of light has been seen traveling in a straight line down the tracks.

Facing north at the crossing where ghost lights have been seen on numerous occasions

There is no reliable documentation of when the ghost lights were first seen. Likewise there are no substantiated cases of violent or sudden death at or near the site to explain the haunting, with one possible exception.

In December, 1940, a mother of two children disappeared from her home near Chapel Hill. Even though she didn't take her children with her, at first it was thought that she was simply off on a holiday vacation. When she didn't come back home after a time, searches commenced with the strong suspicion that she had been murdered. Although no formal accusations had been made, it was suspected that a man who lived close by and who may have been secretly involved with the missing woman was responsible for her disappearance. After she was missing for a couple of weeks, the man committed suicide presumably from strong feelings of guilt. A month later in mid-January her body was found with the help of a psychic from Shelbyville, Tennessee.

In addition to this documented case of murder that happened within the town, there are also two undocumented legends that have passed around concerning decapitations that have occurred on the railroad itself. One was a flagman who ventured too close to the tracks at the crossing. The other concerns a rider who would regularly get off at the crossing as the train slowed. Once a different engineer was in the seat and didn't know to slow at the crossing. The rider jumped anyway and was knocked out by the impact with the metal of the track. A later train not seeing him in time ran over and killed him by decapitation.

The first encounter any of our members had with this ball of light happened in the Fall of 1967. Word had passed around for years (nothing that we knew about had been written at that time) that the railroad at Chapel Hill was haunted. In the parlance of the movie "Animal House" we decided to make a "road trip" to find the ghost. Several of us who were room mates at Middle Tennessee State University chipped in on $2 worth of gas to make the short drive from Murfreesboro. When we arrived at the track, we met another group who got there just ahead of us from the University of Tennessee in Knoxville. News of the railroad track ghost had gotten that far.

These guys had apparently been drinking all the way from Knoxville judging by the way they were acting. So after speaking briefly we walked slowly to let them go up the tracks ahead of us and to get away from us. They were talking loudly and boasting about catching the ghost. At one point they stopped and began throwing rocks off the embankment at the side of the tracks. Suddenly one of them yelled "There it is, and here it comes!" All of them began running toward us at full speed being chased by an orange ball of light about the size of a basketball. After about 25 yards the ball of light simply disappeared, but those guys kept running, jumped into their car, threw gravel as they left, and probably didn't slow until they were safely back in Knoxville.

We lingered around the tracks for a while longer and spotted the ghost lights several more times that night but at a distance and in a variety of colors.

After a lapse of 34 years and with a renewed interest in ghosts, members of our AFFPR Team visited Chapel Hill several times within a relatively short time. On the first occasion four of us went. We walked the tracks for about 100 yards from the crossing in both the north and south directions taking photographs with no results. No lights either visible to the eye or on the digital camera screen showed up. After a short while a train passed traveling north toward Nashville at a fairly fast pace – we estimated the speed at about 70 miles per hour. Since this is a single track that runs about 35 miles to Nashville before splitting, we turned and walked toward the south knowing that another train could not come from behind and surprise us until the first one had reached the split. That would take about 30 or more minutes. We walked for a few minutes and glanced back to see if the ghost lights had reappeared in that direction. Sure enough there in the middle of the track was a large white light, but there was also the distant sound of a train approaching. Only about five minutes had passed, and here was a train traveling in the opposite direction on the same tracks. That means that the first train was not traveling at a mere 70 miles per hour as we had estimated but would have to be moving at a whopping 420 miles per hour to allow what we were witnessing! Were we seeing a phantom train? It looked real enough, but it shouldn't have been there.

Only two of us were able to go on the next trip to the tracks. It was a very dark night with no moon. As we pulled up to the crossing the headlights illuminated a fog that seemed to have gathered only over that spot where the road and the railroad intersected. We parked, got out, walked to the tracks, and right away spotted a small bright light in the distance toward the south. The first thought was that this was a light such as a signal associated with the railroad. The second thought was we don't need any instruments or cameras to see this. It didn't take long to realize that this was no signal. The light moved back and forth, bounced up and down, changed colors from white to blue to red to orange, and at times split into two separate lights. We captured a number of pictures in various juxtapositions during its antics. The screens of our cameras showed more that what we were seeing with our eyes. Two particular photographic anomalies worth noting were (1) an array of many very small lights and (2) ectoplasm reminiscent of a face viewed from the side.

We were facing south from the crossing at Crutcher Road, and the thought occurred to us that perhaps there was another crossing in the direction of the mysterious lights that may be closer to their source. We drove south on US 31 to the next crossing which was about one mile away. As soon as we stepped onto the tracks it became obvious that we were no closer to the light than we were before. This time, however, it appeared about the same size but to the north. So this light that was performing its tricks for us that night emanated from somewhere between the two crossings where there is nothing but a heavily wooded area on both sides of the railroad.

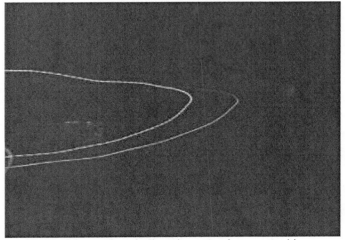

Two power orbs circling the crossing-control box

During the third trip lights were seen from the crossing in both directions. We decided to walk north this time and had one of the strangest encounters of all. From one area (which was probably the same location where the orange ball of light had emerged to chase those college students so many years before) we heard a cacophony of frogs croaking. They sounded like the green tree frogs that are so prevalent and noisy in the South during the warm, humid summer nights. There was one problem. This was January when tree frogs (and all other types of frogs for that matter) are buried deep underground hibernating!

A number of subsequent visits to the Chapel Hill railroad track were made, and never failed to produce some sort of ghostly activity. At least one photograph showed the tracks of three supercharged orbs flying around in the vicinity of the crossing.

Too many have seen and have tried to make sense of these phenomena for too many years to dismiss them lightly. Reports have it that the ball of light has been seen passing through a car stalled on the tracks at one time and through a person standing on the tracks at another time temporarily paralyzing him. One of the locals related a story about how he and a friend taunted the ghost light until it emerged from the side of the tracks and chased them back to their vehicle. Another story has it that a light came and sat on the shoulder of one in the party visiting the tracks.

We may never know who or what this phantom is. Is it the spirit of the young mother who was so brutally murdered there? Is it the flagman who got too close to the tracks? Is it the rider who jumped from the moving train? Is it all of the above? Or is it the remnant of some other life that used to be?

Civil War re-enactors at the Gettysburg Battlefield

Halt! Company!

All of the stories that have been included in this book have been located in the South: mainly Alabama and Tennessee. Certainly Pennsylvania is not a Southern state, but this story has been included because of the large number of ghostly encounters that have been had here, and many of the ghosts are of Southern origin (much to their chagrin) still haunting the Gettysburg battlefield.

On about 15 square miles of mostly farmland in southern Pennsylvania on three hot July days of 1863 two great armies met in the most devastating battle ever fought on American soil. In and around Gettysburg about 70,000 men of the Army of Northern Virginia under General Robert E. Lee and 93,500 men of the Army of the Potomac under Major

146

General George G. Meade clashed. Approximately 50,000 casualties resulted. To put this number in perspective: if the average height of these men was five feet ten inches and they were laid head to toe, the line of bodies would be more than 55 miles long. To say that all 163,500 were men is stretching the truth. Many of the combatants weren't really men at all but mere boys some as young as fifteen.

The three-day battle actually consisted of a number of individual battles and skirmishes that culminated in a final massive assault on July 3 against the main Union force. Devil's Den, the Slaughter Pen, Little Round Top, Round Top, the Triangular Field, Spangler's Spring, and the Wheatfield are only a sampling of the places around the battle arena where major clashes occurred during the three days. Pickett's Charge, the deciding major offensive, consisted of a headlong march by 42 regiments comprising approximately 15,000 Confederates shoulder-to-shoulder across a mile of farmland into the artillery and small-arms fire of 27 regiments comprising approximately 8,000 to 9,000 Union infantry. Whenever artillery rounds from the Union (made up of a mixture of cannonballs and canister which were metal cans that exploded spreading small metal shot over an area thus effectively extending its kill radius), struck the attack line killing several and leaving a hole in the line, the Rebels rapidly closed the line and continued the charge. The charge ended at what has been termed the high-water mark of the Confederacy at a copse of trees used as a landmark toward which Pickett's Charge had aimed. At that point hand-to-hand combat resulted in many more lives lost and a Confederate retreat that ended the battle.

A particular action of interest to us here that occurred near the end of the third day of the battle and involved two battalions of Union cavalry (about 300 men) was led by Brigadier General Elon J. Farnsworth. Farnsworth had only held the rank of General for four days having been promoted on June 30 just prior to the beginning of the battle on July 1. Farnsworth had been ordered by his superior officer Brigadier General Judson Kilpatrick (nicknamed Kill-cavalry) to lead his cavalry to attack a well-protected division of Confederate infantry located on the right flank of the Confederate line. Kilpatrick believed that cavalry could successfully "...fight anywhere but at sea." Farnsworth protested because he would be pitted against an entrenched force over terrain containing fences, boulders, and trees not suitable for a cavalry offensive. He told Kilpatrick that his "...men were too good to die." Kilpatrick was incensed by such a statement that bordered on insubordination and retorted "General Farnsworth, well, somebody can charge!" The message came through loud and clear, and Farnsworth reacted by leading the attack in spite of his best judgment. Farnsworth was killed during the attack by rifle fire from Alabamians who came to help defend that flank.

The area of the battlefield where this event occurred on that hot July 3rd of 1863 is now a quiet, peaceful area along Confederate Avenue. Near the spot where General Farnsworth met his demise is a plaque that describes the action that took place there and the consequences in number of casualties on both sides. A member of the AFFPR present at that site on a very pleasant May afternoon stood listening to the birds signing and the chipmunks playing in the leaves while running a digital recorder. The recorder was allowed to run for about five minutes. The next stop along the chosen route for that day was the Devil's Den at which the same thing was done. This pattern of stopping and running the recorder was followed several times around the battlefield where significant actions had occurred on the fateful three days so many years ago. None of the recordings were reviewed on the battlefield because that precious time out there was needed for recording. Reviewing was to be done later.

Back at the room in the Holiday Inn the recordings were reviewed. Nothing was detected on the first few tracks reviewed except for what sounded like the wind blowing into the microphone. If one listens long enough to this, it would be easy to convince

149

oneself that the wind sounds were actually cannon fire from that long-ago action. After much-too-much listening to nothing the hopes of an EVP being captured by this simple recorder were rapidly waning. However, two minutes and 48 seconds into the fifth recording which was at the site of Farnsworth's cavalry battle a loud bugle blast came through followed by a Union commander's voice ordering "HALT, COMPANY!" Sleep was not a luxury to be had that night. Imagine capturing a voice from a battle that had occurred nearly 140 years ago. Obviously the battle is still being fought by all those "good men" as General Farnsworth had referred to them.

One of the Confederate cannons used in the battle

Could the three-second recording of a bugle and the voice actually be that of General

Farnsworth? Unfortunately for those of us who would like to know, there will never be a way of knowing. Since the words were "HALT, COMPANY," maybe it was really one of the company commanders within the two battalions of Vermont horse soldiers that Farnsworth led.

Mark Nesbitt in his series of books *The Ghosts of Gettysburg* has chronicled a good many stories of ghostly encounters on this famous battlefield. Sightings of full-body apparitions, orbs, ectoplasm, and vortexes are common in and around the area. There are of course a good many hypotheses about what ghosts are and why they exist. The most popular idea espoused by many researchers in the field is that ghosts are the souls of those who have met tragic, sudden and unexpected death or those who have very compelling unfinished business. The spirits of the young especially after a sudden death are confused as to what happened to them and where they are. The presence of strong emotions such as love and hate also seem to be involved in paranormal phenomena. How often are ghost stories told that relate how young lovers were forever separated by no fault of their own to be ultimately driven to suicide only to wind up haunting the place of their demise?

Mentioned previously many of the men who were killed during this three-day hell on Earth were quite young, killed in their prime.

Probably many were dispatched to the afterlife with many of the usual unfinished businesses of life. It would appear that the theories certainly fit the evidence considering the tremendous of life that occurred on this famous battlefield that provided opportunities for the presence of spirits.

The Wheatfield is another one of those areas within the battle arena where a significant number of soldiers were killed. On July 2 the Union soldiers clashed with the Confederates in an open triangular-shaped field that was about 400 yards on each side. The field was being used at the time by a local farmer to grow wheat. Except for a rock fence on the eastern side of the field little or no protection was afforded to any of the combatants. Typical of the entire Gettysburg engagement the losses were enormous. The 1st Minnesota regiment of Harrow's brigade for example suffered a lost of 82 percent of its men during the fracas. One observer commenting on the appearance of the field after the battle stated that instead of brown with wheat it was now blue referring to the large numbers of Union soldiers lying dead or wounded there.

The Wheatfield is now as with the rest of the area a peaceful open field tended by the National Park Service. However, to many who have cared to look deeper and to many unsuspecting visitors, restless spirits of those who departed this life on July 2, 1863 have made themselves known in various ways. During the International Ghost Hunters Society annual Gettysburg Conference in May, 2002, several attendees spent an evening until the Park closed at 10:00 pm in the Wheatfield. Spaced out over the field attempting to detect the presence of the many spirits known to haunt that place, the IGHS members were armed with the usual array of equipment: cameras, video cameras, and recorders. No one was disappointed. However, each one experienced the presence of the spirits in different ways. Walking around the battlefield several cold spots were detected not by thermal scanners but simply by walking through the space and feeling the chill. Speaking of being chilled, one young lady there shared an EVP that she had obtained the night before. Sitting alone in the field she asked the question: "Is there anyone here who would like to speak to me?" An immediate answer came through: "SO MANY!" Hearing this drawn out whispery voice chilled us all to the bone.

Armed only with a digital camera that night the member of the AFFPR who attended the Conference photographed an interesting sight at the southeastern side of the Wheatfield that abutted the forest. Just as dark began to descend a very bright orb showed up in the camera screen. Another quick shot captured the orb as having moved about 25 feet from where it was. Another shot showed it had moved approximately 25 feet more, and was being followed by a second orb. Successive shots showed the two orbs following or maybe chasing each other around the field until both disappeared. The entire scene developed over a span of eight photographs taken in rapid succession.

Many individual battles were fought over the span of this 15 square miles to comprise the Battle of Gettysburg climaxing with Pickett's Charge. All of the areas have been found by paranormal investigators to have spirits of the men who died there and others, some identified and some not. The areas reported to be haunted are:

Devil's Den	Culp's Hill
Little Round Top	Peach Orchard
Wheatfield	Triangular Field
Slaughter Pen	Seminary Ridge
Barlow Knoll	East Cemetery Hill
High Water Mark	Rose Woods
Spangler's Spring	Lee's Headquarters
Valley of Death	Reynold's Woods
East Cavalry Field	Cashtown Inn
Sachs Bridge	Pardee Field

And all of the field hospitals located in homes and buildings in and around the battlefield.

There is no doubt as to why the Gettysburg Battlefield is labeled as the most haunted single site in the United States. There

154

are so many souls there who have been destined to refight this battle over and over throughout the intervening 140 years since it was first fought on those sultry summer days of July, 1863. We can only pray that one day they will all find peace, and once again join as brothers.

Conclusion

As proclaimed in the preface this has been a great ride. We truly hope that you have enjoyed reading about these real ghostly encounters as much as we have enjoyed experiencing them. The sheer number of hauntings that are apparently out there is so large that in a relatively short period of time the AFFPR has had the privilege of experiencing most of the phenomena that have been documented as being associated with ghosts. Of course being at the right place with the right instruments, the right attitude, and armed with the right background information is critical to a successful ghost hunt.

The right instruments to "see" and "hear" ghosts have been enumerated several times throughout the narrative of this text. However, to reiterate this list the members of the AFFPR use:
- Video cameras
- 35 mm cameras
- Digital cameras

- Night vision scopes
- Audio tape recorders
- Remote microphones
- Digital sound recorders
- Thermal meters
- EMF detectors

All of the cameras in the list are capable of seeing what cannot be seen by the unaided eye. The video tape with its magnetic coating, 35 mm film, instant film, and the digital camera all can detect somewhat into the near infrared portion of the electromagnetic spectrum where most of the "visible" ghostly evidence is obtainable. With these devices we have been able to tape and/or photograph orbs (both stationary and in motion), ectoplasm, vortexes (including shadows cast by them), shadows, and apparitions most of which could not be seen at the time they were being photographed or taped.

Since the near infrared wavelengths are those most often encountered, night vision scopes are ideal for witnessing the same phenomena as with the camera but without the permanency of recording the event.

Remote-sensing thermometers detect the changes in temperature that sometimes accompany spirits. Generally drops in temperature indicate an endothermic phenomenon (i.e. the spirit absorbs heat energy from its surroundings). Hot spots have also been reported, but we have not experienced them in our investigations.

The EMF detector is commonly used for detecting electromagnetic fields associated with electrical/electronic devices and electrical conductors under a load. Some ghostly phenomena are detectable by the electromagnetic field they have but only when they are in close proximity.

Digital sound recorders have proved invaluable in our investigations. As indicated throughout the book we have recorded EVP's with a number of messages from the spirit world. Most are cryptic and not easily understood within the context of our knowledge. On the other hand many are direct responses to questions or situations at the given moment. Two ideas have been proposed to explain the ability to record what we cannot hear. One is that the sounds are below the range of human hearing in the infrasonic frequency band (<20 db). It follows that the recorder can pick up the magnetic record of these sounds. It would seem that if this is true, the recordings would be awfully noisy considering the background when in fact many are quite clear. The second opinion is that the sounds are generated in such a way as to be recordable on the magnetic medium but do not cause a vibration in the ear as normal sound does.

Being in the right place is certainly of prime importance. Most of the places that we investigate have long histories of being haunted. The ghosts on the Chapel Hill, Tennessee railroad track for example have been seen by hundreds of people over many years. A few of the places that we have investigated have not been previously reported but usually a great deal of paranormal activity has occurred there to warrant an investigation.

The right attitude is important to a successful hunt. It is ok to have a healthy skepticism but not a negative one. As stated from the beginning we have reviewed and re-reviewed our findings to ensure that there were no false reports within this book. At times during our hunts we thought that we had EVP's saying various odd things. When we scrutinized them carefully, however, several were discarded as explainable. For example an EVP that we thought said "CHAINS" turned out to be a deep sign that one person emitted when sitting down after a couple of hours standing in a cemetery recording and photographing.

Finally the right background information on the haunted location is important to the hunt. A history of the building or site and what happened there enables us to focus on the areas where the ghosts reside. Certainly this improves our chances of success. Also the history allows us to ask the right questions in our efforts to elicit EVP's. Typical questions vary with the location but generally follow:

- Is anyone here?
- What is your name?
- Do you wish to speak to us?
- How old are you?
- What year is it?
- Do you like this place?
- Are you in any pain?
- Are you scared?
- Do you have a message for us?
- Do you want us to leave?

Intermingled with these questions are those more specific to the situation. For example for ghosts of children we might ask "What games do you like to play?" For ghosts of Native Americans we might ask "May we sit by your fire?" The right background information is also invaluable in accurately documenting the haunting as we have attempted to do so in this work.

In conclusion if there is a haunted site particularly in Alabama, Tennessee, Georgia, or Mississippi that needs to be investigated for the paranormal activity there, the AFFPR is available. Any of the following e-mail addresses may be used to contact us. Please include whatever background information that you might have on the site as well as your relationship to the owners.

bamaghosthunter@hotmail.com
Nest9@yahoo.com

rvnixon@knology.net

Happy hunting!

<u>Glossary</u>

Apparition – a manifestation of a spirit usually having discernable human features. It can be full-body, partial-body, transparent/translucent, or solid.   Sometimes only the shape is of a human form, and individual features such as those of the face are hazy.

Audible sound – sound in the frequency range of 20 – 20,000 hertz that can be detected with the unaided ear.

Cold spot – a space wherein a noticeable drop in temperature occurs.   The location of an invisible spirit can often be detected by remote-sensing thermometers that sense a space colder than its surroundings.

Ectoplasm – a manifestation of a spirit that appears as a haze or mist sometimes having human-like characteristics.

Electromagnetic field intensity – the strength of the electric/magnetic field at a given point. This type of energy is sometimes associated with the presence of a spirit. The intensity can be determined by the appropriate instrument to pinpoint the location of the spirit.

Electromagnetic radiation – energy that includes visible light, ultraviolet light, infrared light, microwaves, and others. Spirits not in the visible-light portion of the spectrum can occasionally be seen with devices capable of "seeing" in the near infrared (>400 nanometers) portion of the spectrum.

Electronic voice phenomenon (EVP) – communicating spirits not heard as audible sound can sometimes be recorded on either magnetic tape (tape recorder) or by a digital recorder which also records magnetically. This is becoming a very popular method for detecting the presence of spirits.

Endothermic reaction – a phenomenon which involves the absorption of heat energy from the surroundings thus creating a drop in temperature.

Frequency – in the sense herein used frequency is the number of wavelengths that move past a given point in a given amount of time, typically one second. Electromagnetic waves (light) and sound waves have frequencies that are detectable by normal sight and hearing. Frequencies outside these normal ranges are those often encountered with spirits.

Ghost – the term used to refer to an apparition or to unexplained happenings within a space.

Imprint – a moment in time which a spirit is forced to repeat over and over. An example would be that of an apparition which appears at one end of a hall, walks to the other end, and disappears. This scene would then be reenacted many times without varying.

Infrared radiation – electromagnetic radiation that is just beyond the visible red portion of the spectrum. The wavelengths are longer and the frequencies lower than visible light. Infrared light can be made visible by use of night-vision scopes.

Orb or Spirit Orb – mostly round, transparent lights usually not visible with the unaided eye associated with spirits of the dead. These lights can be "seen" by night-vision scopes, 35 mm film cameras, digital cameras, and infrared cameras. This is the most common manifestation of a spirit.

Paranormal – events out of the ordinary that are not part of this plane of existence.

Parapsychology – the science of studying the paranormal; also includes the study of such phenomena as ESP, telekinesis, out-of-body experiences, etc.

Poltergeist – a word of German origin meaning a noisy ghost. This is used to describe any type of paranormal phenomena that involves objects moving, falling, breaking, etc. Also used to describe unexplained noises whether involving real objects or not.

Portal – thought to be an opening into another dimension. This is a space where one's personal energy is rapidly drained.

Sensory detection – that which can be seen, heard, felt, tasted, or smelled by the ordinary senses.

Shadow people – those in the spirit realm who appear as shadows often with somewhat human form. May be visible with the eye or more often via camera or video camera.

Spirit – the essence of the departed soul. Can manifest itself as an orb, ectoplasm, a vortex, or an apparition. Also it can be present but undetectable.

Super-charged Orb – a very fast moving orb. These have been photographed numerous times and appear in a picture as a bright light at the end of a line of light. The line is actually the path of travel during the time the camera shutter is open.

Visible radiation – that part of the electromagnetic spectrum that can be seen by the unaided eye. The various wavelengths make up the colors of the spectrum which are from low to high wavelength: violet, indigo, blue, green, yellow, orange, and red. All of these colors together yield white light.

Vortex – the manifestation of a spirit that appears as a swirling column of light. These are often seen in photographs when they were invisible to the naked eye.

References

The Natives of Russell Cave

Griffin, J.W., *Investigations in Russell Cave*, National Park Service-U.S. Department of the Interior, 1974.

Miller, C. and B. Honeycutt, "Life 8,000 Years Ago Uncovered in an Alabama Cave," *National Geographic Magazine*, Volume CX, Number 4, October, 1956.

A Witch in Tennessee?

Bell, C.B. and H.P. Miller, *The Bell Witch of Tennessee*, 1934.

Ingram, M.V., *Authenticated History of the Bell Witch and Other Stories of the World's*

Greatest Unexplained Phenomenon, Clarksville, Tennessee, 1894.

Price, C.E., *The Infamous Bell Witch of Tennessee*, The Overmountain Press, Johnson City, Tennessee, 1994.

Taylor, T., *Season of the Witch, The Haunted History of the Bell Witch of Tennessee*, Whitechapel Productions, Alton, Illinois, 1999.

Weathered Stones and Spirits
Chamberlain, D., *Storied Ground*, Fell House Publishing, Huntsville, Alabama, 1997.

Dooling, D. and S. Dooling, *Huntsville, A Pictorial History*, Donning Company, VA, 1980.

The Railroad Track Ghost of Chapel Hill
Windham, K.T., *13 Tennessee Ghosts and Jeffery*, The University of Alabama Press, Tuscaloosa, Alabama, 1977.

Halt! Company!
Cotton, B., *Gettysburg: The Final Fury*, Doubleday & Company, Inc., Garden City, New York, 1974.

Nesbitt, M., *Ghosts of Gettysburg*, Thomas of Gettysburg, PA, 1991.

Storrick, W.C., *The Battle of Gettysburg*, J. Horace McFarland Company, Harrisburg, PA, 1931.

Trudeau, N.A., *Gettysburg, A Testing of Courage*, Harper Collins Publishers, Inc., New York, 2002.

ISBN 1553951131-1

9 781553 951131